Learning More About Your Ancestors Online

Genealogy Guides for Newbies, Hobbyists, and Old Pros

By Kenneth R. Marks

Notifications

Background: These genealogy guides are compiled here as a convenient collection to help you find greater success and pleasure in your genealogy pursuits. They were originally introduced by the author for his website TheAncestorHunt.com and have been significantly upgraded and enhanced for this publication. These easy-to-use materials will start or continue you on your way to becoming a more successful researcher in all kinds of genealogical record categories.

References: Mention of third parties or third-party products within this publication is for informational purposes only and constitutes neither a recommendation nor an endorsement. Internet addresses and related resources referenced in this book are accurate at the time of publication; however, the publisher does not endorse them or vouch for their content or permanence.

Legal: All information in this book is deemed accurate and reliable as of the date of publication. However, neither the publisher nor the author assumes any responsibility for the validity, use, or misuse of any information contained in this publication; and makes no warranties regarding the results of use of information herein. The views expressed in this book are the opinion of the author; the reader is responsible for his or her own actions.

Respect: No part of this publication may be reproduced without written consent of the author. Please do not steal. All trademarks appearing in this book are the property of their respective owners.

Table of Contents

7. Miscellaneous

8. Newspaper Research

9. Occupations

10. Photographs and Physical Description

11. Residences and Other Locations

12. Schools and Yearbooks

13. Resources

Index

1. Introduction

Help your ancestors live forever…
Write their family history.

About the Author

My name is Kenneth R Marks, and I reside in Arizona. And below is the story of how I began the journey of finding my family history.

In 2002, for a reason long forgotten, I joined ancestry.com as a "free subscriber." Not driven by a passion to "know" my roots, but just interested, I began the search.

When I started, knew the first and last names of only two of my great grandparents – both on my Mother's side of the family. I did remember Grandpa Heyman, my father's grandfather, but didn't know his first name. All five of my remaining great grandparents were a total mystery to me. In fact, I have no memory of anyone in my family even mentioning them – not necessarily because they led "bad" lives or had a sordid history – just because no one talked of them.

My dear mother passed in July 2003. After her passing, I became more interested, again not a passion but just interest. You might ask "Did you ask your Mother about any family history between 2002 and the date of her passing?" And the answer is NO! Ask the living before it is too late. Ask about their lives and their stories. And don't just look at their photo books, ask them about the people who are in these albums. And for gosh sake, write the names and locations of the photos down.

Since that time, I have become an obsessed Ancestor Hunter. The Ancestor Hunt website was created about a decade ago to "help people find stuff." In a nutshell, we find links to Free Online Collections, so that you can use them. What started as 10,000 links to Free Online Newspaper Titles in 2014 has blossomed to over 160,000 links in 20 different Genealogy Record Collection categories. In addition, we also write about tools and techniques that we have discovered over the years that are extremely helpful in genealogy research.

This is one of my favorite ancestor photos, taken 100 years ago:
"The Leo Metzner and Martha Heyman Wedding"
including the Braunhart, Heyman, and Marks Families.
My grandmother and my father as an infant are on the right.

Another of my favorite ancestor photos, taken 120 years ago in Schubin,
Germany. Five immigrated to America and two died in the Holocaust.

Getting Started

Early on in my genealogical journey, I discovered a variety of techniques that made my searching easier and more successful. In the beginning, I documented those techniques in blog posts on my website. In the last two years, I summarized some of those techniques and other useful genealogy research tips in what I call Quick Sheets, commonly known as Quick Reference Guides. Most were just one page. I have used those tips and techniques blog posts, and the Sheets and Guides, as the basis for this book, enhancing each of them significantly as they were consolidated here. And several are new.

If you are new to genealogy, this book will serve to introduce you to information that otherwise you might take years to discover on your own.

If you have greater experience, this information can serve as a reminder of things to look for, especially if you are working on a genealogy category that you do not research very often.

In all cases, hopefully this book can be part of your genealogy reference collection and help you with your research.

I wish you great success and satisfaction in your journey through history, learning more about your personal ancestry and genealogy.

2. Birth and Marriage

A marriage isn't a marriage unless there is a ceremony. A marriage announcement, license, or engagement party does not mean they got married.

32 Ways to Find Ancestor Birth Information

- **Birth Announcements in Newspapers:** Older ones in the Vitals section say "To the wife of John Smith, a son, in Marysville on Wednesday" or something like that. You can calculate based on the date of the newspaper the exact birth date. There are also birth announcements in the local news and society page sections.

- **Birth Certificates:** This is the best document for establishing date and location of birth. Usually, they are signed by an attending physician who was there when the baby was born; at least for those in the last several decades.

- **Cemetery Records:** There are lots of different ways to find this information. On a headstone the date of birth (often only the year) is inscribed. And you can visit individual cemeteries where burial records sometimes are made available. But these are only as good as the information that the purchaser of the gravestone has provided. Mistakes can be made.

- **Census Records:** Well, you won't find anyone's birth dates in most census records (except you can get the birth month and year in the 1900 U.S. Census). But you do get the age stated and that could lead you to a possible birth year within 1, 2, or 3 years.

- **Church Records:** Baptism and christening records and similar records for other faiths may include birth dates or the date of the event, from which you might be able to calculate the birth date. You might want to keep track of what churches, synagogues, etc. that your ancestors and their families worshiped.

- **Death Certificates:** Often the date of birth is included in the death certificate, if not the actual date but at least the age at the person's passing so the year can be calculated. But again, the information is only as good as the memory or knowledge of the informant.

- **Divorce Records:** At least the age is included if not the birth information.

- **Draft Cards:** The applicant must enter their exact birth date.

- **Employment and Union Records:** Hard to find but may include date of birth

- **Employment Records:** Job applications and other employment files may include the date of birth.

- **Funeral and Memorial Records/Books:** Often the deceased's birth date is included in the memorial cards or books. Also, the records from the funeral home, may include date information.

- **Great Registers:** Used for voting primarily in the 1800s, the age of the voter is included so you will have to use your math and subtraction skills to ascertain the approximate birth year.

- **Hospital Records:** Might be useful if accurate records were maintained and made accessible years after the birth.

- **Immigration Records:** Although the exact birth date is not often included, the age is, so simple math, like with census records, can get you within a year or so for the birth year.

- **Marriage Licenses and Announcements:** Usually the age of the applicant is listed in the newspaper and on the license itself, so again simple math can lead you to the birth year.

- **Membership Organizations:** Unions, fraternities/sororities, lodges, clubs, etc. may include the date of birth in application information.

- **Military Records:** The military is quite good at keeping lots of information regarding service members, so you should have lots of places where the birth information is recorded, especially in enlistment papers.

- **Motor Vehicle Department Records:** If retained, at least the age if not the birth date of the driver will be included.

- **Naturalization and Citizenship Records:** Exact birth dates are included.

- **Newsletters and Minutes:** Organizations, clubs, churches, and other types of organizations often publish or recognize birthdays for members, which sometimes may include the year of birth as well.

- **Obituaries:** Might include the actual birth date and location, if not just the age. It seems that more recent online tributes contain the actual date, while older newspaper obituaries more than likely do not.

- **Passport Applications:** The date of birth is included in many variations of applications for passports.

- **Pension Records:** Whether military or civilian, birth date and location may be included.

- **Personal Bibles:** Many families recorded birth and death date information in the family Bible.

- **Personal Testimony:** Often used in obtaining a Delayed Registration of Birth when no official record was created at the actual time of birth.

- **School Records:** Enrollment records may include the date of birth.

- **Social Security Applications:** The birth date is always requested in the SS-5 application.

- **Social Security Death Index (SSDI):** The date of birth is included in the SSDI.

- **State Birth and Death Indexes:** Whether online or in a book at a library/archive, these provide dates and sometimes the location of the birth. But since they are indexes that were most likely entered from birth certificates, hospital reports, or death indexes, you always must keep in mind that transcription and typing errors can occur.

- **Town Records:** Most often in the New England states, but also in others, towns maintained vital statistic information and published them in annual Town Reports.

- **Travel Records:** Although these are sometimes called immigration records, many in the 1900s indeed does have the actual birth date of the traveler.

- **Wills and Estate Files:** Age and possibly birth information is included. Probate court documents may provide fruitful.

27 Ways to Find Ancestor Marriage Information

- **Cemetery Records:** Although dates and location of marriage are not included, many times husband and wife are buried next to each other, so if you did not know a person was married—look at the person next to them; if they are the same name they might have been married to that person, so at least you can get more clues. This may seem obvious but depending on how the naming was engraved; it may have been a son or brother. Also, interment cards and plot deeds may reference a married couple.

- **Census Records:** Well, you won't find anyone's marriage dates in census records. But that "M" or "S" will indicate if they are married or single. And even a "W" for widowed, or "D" for divorced will tell you if they were married. Often an "M1" or M2" will indicate whether they are on their first or second marriage. Questions such as "years married" or "age at first marriage" are helpful for tracking down marriage dates.

- **Church Records:** Just as churches maintain birth and christening records, marriage records are also often available.

- **City Directories:** Often city directories include the first name of the spouse of the person, and if the person is widowed, the name of the deceased spouse.

- **Cohabitation Registers:** For marriages and children born to those in slavery.

- **Consent Papers:** Generally required if the bride or groom was underage. Usually kept with the marriage license by the local government entity.

- **Court Records:** May include spouses names, and possibly widow or widower's name.

- **Death Certificates:** The marital status is included as well as the name of the surviving spouse, but not the date of marriage or how many years they were married.

- **Divorce Records:** Dates and locations of marriage are included in divorce records. Divorce indexes are usually not as detailed, as they often do not include the actual marriage date, but only the number of years married.

- **Dowry and Pre-nuptial Documents:** The name of the spouse and often date and location of marriage is included. I have a dowry document from the 1800s that includes this information.

- **Draft Cards:** The applicant enters a contact person and often parenthetically enters the word "wife." No marriage dates or locations but at least an indication that they were married, and the given name of his wife will be helpful for further research,

- **Immigration and Travel Records:** Often the "Married or Single" question is included so at least their marital status is indicated.

- **Land Deeds:** May identify spouse if both parties' names are on the deed.

- **Marriage Banns:** Recorded announcements of intended marriages are often maintained by churches and town records.

- **Marriage Bonds:** Written guarantees or promises of payment made by the groom or another person.

- **Marriage Certificates:** This is the best document for establishing date and location of the marriage. Usually, they are completed and signed by the person performing the ceremony. Often, they were called "Marriage Returns" when the officiant "returned" the signed certificate.

- **Marriage Indexes:** Whether online or in a book at a library or archive, these provide dates and the location of marriage. But since they are indexes that are most likely entered from marriage certificates, you always must keep in mind that transcription and typing errors can occur.

- **Marriage Licenses and Other Announcements in the Newspaper:** Marriage license announcements, as well as weddings and engagements abound in newspapers. Tons of marriage related information can be found in newspapers, in the vitals section, society pages, women's sections as well as the local interest sections.

- **Marriage Licenses:** These are tricky because they do not evidence that a wedding actually occurred, so further research is required to ascertain that fact. Please notice that on many licenses it indicates the number of previous marriages for the individual. On several occasions I have found that ancestors had previously been married, which was a total surprise to me.

- **Military Records:** For next of kin information, the spouse's name and contact information is included, if not the actual dates and location of marriage.

- **Naturalization Records:** Exact marriage dates are included.

- **Newspaper Obituaries:** Sometimes, the date of marriage was included in the written obituary printed in newspapers.

- **Passport Applications:** The name of a married woman's husband is included for early 20th century passports. And sometimes, place and date of marriage is included.

- **Pension Applications:** Military or not, evidence of marriage is required for beneficiary certification, so a copy of the marriage certificate is required.

- **Personal Bibles:** Many families recorded marriage date information in the family Bible.

- **Personal Collections:** Wedding invitations, wedding programs, and personal letters citing a family wedding.

- **Wills and Probate Documents:** Although dates and location of marriages are not often included, at least the name of the spouse is available.

Notes

3. Death Records and Information

We spend a lot of our research time trying to find the story of our ancestor's lives. It is also important to discover the story of our ancestor's deaths.

15 Reasons to Research Funeral and Memorial Books

There are a bunch of different documents and records that the genealogist and family historian can utilize to find out more about one's ancestors, no matter whether they be related to life event dates or locations or include other information. I have found that funeral and memorial books hold a ton of interesting information, much more so than one might initially consider. Some memorial books are quite ornate, and leather bound, but many are quite simple and have less than 6 pages (at least the ones from the mid to late 20th century for my family).

Here is a list of the types of information that are almost always included in these pamphlets and books:

- **Name of the Deceased:** Often the complete name including middle name is provided. For women, sometimes the maiden name and married name is written, but sometimes just the married surname.

- **Birth Date**

- **Birth Location**

- **Death Date**

- **Death Location**

- **Age:** Often expressed in years, months, and days.

- **Parents Names**

- **Grandparents Names**

- **Members of the Deceased's Family:** Usually very helpful information, especially if there is no obituary.

- **Obituary:** I have one memorial for my great grandmother that has her obituary pasted in the memorial book.

- **Location of Services**

- **Officiating Clergy**

- **Place of Interment**

- **Date of Interment**

- **Friends and Flowers:** This is the "holy grail" in my opinion for information in these books. If you are familiar with collateral research and especially Elizabeth Shown Mills' FANs (Friends, Associates, and Neighbors), you know how useful this research can be. Also, you know that having these people's names listed as attendees at a funeral service mean that somehow, they knew the deceased. Maybe they were a co-worker, or a neighbor, or a relative or friend of one of the deceased's children. That information is certainly useful when trying to find a census record when the deceased's last name has been butchered by the census taker or the indexer. Maybe for land plats they were their neighbors as well. Maybe by researching a co-worker you can discover their occupation. And lots of other "side-door" research and analysis of these names may bear fruit on the actual person that you are researching.

Beyond all this information – Maybe their favorite hymns were sung. Also, one or two of their favorite poems were included in the book. All of this adds richness to our understanding of the life of the deceased – not just the dates and typical family tree information.

24 Ways to Find Ancestor Death Information

- **Alumni Directories and Newsletters:** For both high school and college graduates, may contain a notice about the death of a former student.

- **Cemetery and Burial Records:** There are lots of ways to find this information. There are several online sites that have information and photos of gravestones, where the date (or at least year) of death is inscribed. And you can visit individual cemeteries where records sometimes are made available. But again, these are only as good as the information that the purchaser of the gravestone has provided. Many cemeteries have online burial indexes now. Burial permits may have been kept as well and will be useful.

- **Census Records:** Well, you won't find anyone's death dates in a census record. But you might find some clues. Say Mr. Smith and his family showed up in the 1930 census. But in the 1940 census, the same family is there but he isn't. If he had died, likely Mrs. Smith would be denoted with a "W" or Wd" in the Marital Status column indicating that she was a widow. Remember to search the Census Mortality schedules if available.

- **Church Newsletters:** I have found ancestor death dates in newsletters for the Church that they attended. So, for more recent deaths for churches that write and distribute newsletters - this is a source of death date clues. You might want to keep track of what churches, synagogues, etc. that your ancestors worshipped.

- **Church Records:** If the funeral or memorial services were held in the church, records will; be kept, especially if there is an attached cemetery. And burial records were kept for associated cemeteries.

- **City Directories:** You won't find death dates in City Directories either, but if Mr. Smith showed up in a 1922 City Directory with his wife's name in parentheses, e.g., "(Polly)" and then the 1923 City Directory has no Mr. Smith and a Polly Smith (widow) at the same address, then you might conclude that Mr. Smith died in 1922 or 1923. Some directories listed residents as "deceased".

- **Coroner's Reports:** Although a coroner's report often states the date the deceased person was found, which may have been different than when he or she died, the reports are quite detailed and can provide quite useful information.

- **Death Records and Certificates:** This is the best document for establishing date and location of death. Usually, they are signed by an attending physician (at least in the last 100 years or so) who was there when the ancestor patient died. But other information on the certificate is only as good as the information known and memory of the informant, usually a family member.

- **Family Histories and Biographies:** Many times, the deceased and/or family may donate family records and possibly biographies to the local library. Finding these can be a gold mine.

- **Immigration Records:** In the oft chance where an ancestor died while immigrating, make sure that you check all the pages of a recorded voyage. Many times, there are notes, should the immigrant have passed while in transit.

- **Land Records:** Sales of land or transfers of ownership from the deceased to the living spouse can sometimes give you an estimated death date, from which you might be able to ascertain exact information from other records.

- **Military Records:** The military is quite good in keeping lots of information regarding service members, so you should have lots of places where the death information is recorded, in the case of an ancestor who died while on active duty.

- **Mortuary Records:** This is a resource that I have personally used. Often, they are hard to get to, but they often provide a great deal of information regarding the decedent and his or her burial and funeral, including date of death. And some of the mortuary records have the obituary attached.

- **Newspaper Legal Notices:** About the estate, disposition of the estate, etc.

- **Newspaper Local Interest Articles:** In smaller, local newspapers, often the goings on from residents and guests were recorded. If someone traveled to or from the town to attend a funeral, often the deceased's name was mentioned.

- **Obituaries, Obituary Indexes and Newspaper Death Notices:** Another very frequently used piece of information. But these are only as good as the memory of the person providing the information, as well as the person working at the newspaper and their skill and attention to detail. Many mistakes are made in obituaries.

- **Pension Records:** Whether military or civilian, death date and location may be included.

- **Personal Bibles:** Many families recorded birth and death date information in the family Bible.

- **Private Death Records:** Includes insurance papers, medical records, etc.

- **Probate, Wills and Estates:** These legal documents will likely have the death information for your ancestor who has passed, as well as the legal proceedings and will information.

- **SSDI:** The Social Security Death Index (SSDI) is probably the most frequently researched collection of death information. Unfortunately, there are many instances of errors and omissions evident in this collection. Often only the month of last benefit is entered rather than the death date. And the location is the location where benefits were received - not always the actual death location. The Social Security NUMIDENT Files from the U.S. National Archives are also quite useful.

- **State Death Indexes:** Whether online or in a book at a library, these provide dates and sometimes locations of death. But since they are indexes that are most likely entered from death certificates, you always must keep in mind that transcription and typing errors can occur.

- **Tax Records:** Sometimes records might list someone as deceased but may by implication (the person is missing), indicate that the person died or moved.

- **Town Records:** Most often in the New England states, but also in others, towns maintained vital statistic information and published them in annual Town Reports.

24 Cemetery Records besides Tombstone Inscriptions

Cemetery records and cemeteries in general are a very large part of our family history and are a significant pursuit for many genealogists. Sometimes, the information on a headstone is the only information available for certain ancestors.

There are different types of cemeteries. Just being buried in a specific cemetery may provide a clue to ethnicity, religion, military status, or lodge association.

- **Church Cemetery:** Owned and managed by a church. May be on church grounds or nearby.

- **Commercial Cemetery:** For profit cemeteries. May be owned or affiliated with a funeral home or mortuary.

- **Ethnic Cemetery:** Provided to support a specific religion or ethnicity.

- **Family Cemetery:** Usually located on land owned by a family; may have multiple generations of family members interred.

- **Mass Grave:** A common grave for multiple people; generally, the indigent or those who perished in a disaster.

- **Military Cemetery:** Reserved for veterans and possibly their spouse.

- **Public Cemetery:** Typically owned and operated by a city or county.

The tombstone often provides more information than just the name of the deceased, the birth date and/or year, and the death date and/or year. Also, there is a lot of information "behind the scenes" that can be very valuable in your research.

What might we find in cemetery records?

- **Age at death**

- **Burial Permit**

- **Cause of death**

- **Copy of the death certificate**

- **Copy of the obituary**

- **Cost of the plot and/or burial**

- **Full birth and/or death dates, including locations**

- **Full name, including maiden name for women**

- **Location of plot; on plot map**

- **Location of the plot in Plot map**

- **Marital status**

- **Military affiliation**

- **Military service, religion, occupation, or membership in an organization.**

- **Name of doctor and/or hospital**

- **Name of officiating minister or clergyman**

- **Names of other persons related to the deceased,**

- **Names of others involved (e.g., mortuary, headstone company)**

- **Plot deed**

- **Plot Maps:** includes grave locations and plot ownership

- **Prior residence address of the deceased**

- **Tombstone decorations:** sometimes include symbols or words about occupations, membership in fraternal organizations or churches.

- **Tombstone Inscriptions:** birth and death dates. May contain relationships to parents, spouses, and children.

- **Transfer to or from that cemetery**

- **Where deceased died, if different from residence**

- **Who else is buried in the plot**

25 Reasons to Research Probate Records and Wills

Does the thought of locating and searching through old probate records and wills turn you off, because you will need to go through some court's smelly basement, where you must pore through dusty old files of records? Let me tell you, whether you have to find them that way or online, they are incredibly valuable sources of information about the deceased. They are often well documented and provide a ton of details about the deceased's life activities, relationships, relatives, friends, and acquaintances.

Here is a list of just some of the information available in Probate Records and Wills.

- **Adoptions and/or Guardianships**

- **Businesses Owned:** If a partnership business arrangement existed., the names of the partners would be listed.

- **Children's Names:** And possibly their birth date and location

- **Children's Spouses' Names**

- **Citizenship Status:** And possibly naturalization information.

- **Date and Location of Death**

- **Deaths of Other Family Members:** Possibly including siblings and children, or parents, depending on the age of the deceased

- **Debts of the Deceased**

- **Deceased's Signature:** If on a will

- **Executor/Trustee for the Estate:** And alternates if the Trustee is deceased

- **Feelings of the Deceased toward Family Members:** This can be deduced if not stated explicitly, by the amount of the estate that is bequeathed in relation to that of others

- **Full Name:** Often the middle name is a challenge to find while researching, but it likely is found in either the will or probate documents

- **Grandchildren's Names**

- **Guardianship of Minor Children:** If both parents are deceased

- **Household Items**

- **Inventory of items Owned by the Deceased**

- **Name of Spouse:** And likely ex-spouses if they were a parent of your children

- **Occupations**

- **Other Heirs:** May be nieces or nephews, and close friends or associates, as well as home workers, if the deceased employed them.

- **Real Estate Property Owned:** Including their locations and value.

- **Residences:** This may include old residences and possibly those of their children.

- **Siblings**

- **Specific Bequests:** If not to a person specifically; may be to a charity, or church, or other organization; may also specify an amount for care of a minor child

- **Wills of Slaveholders:** May name slaves owned

- **Witnesses to the Signing of the Will**

32 Reasons Why Searching Obituaries is Like Finding Gold

Make the most of what is written in an obituary; look for the information below; and analyze each and every word carefully. Personally, my biggest research breakthrough was because of an obituary in a newspaper.

- **Age:** This is usually a part of an obit, even though it should never be construed as an exact age, even in years.

- **Awards:** Whether occupational or otherwise, adds depth to the deceased's life story.

- **Birth Date**

- **Birth Location:** Be careful with these; although they typically state the actual location, "native of" should not be construed as the actual birth location.

- **Burial Information:** Name of cemetery is likely included. None of course, if cremated. Notice a Neptune Society reference which implies that her ashes may have been "buried" at sea.

- **Cause of Death**

- **Church Membership:** Terrific information if one wants to contact the church for additional information

- **College Degrees and Professional Certifications**

- **Death Date:** Based on the publication date of the newspaper, sometimes the exact date is listed or the day of the week so you can calculate the date of death.

- **Death Information of Others:** "...brother of the 'late' so and so." Indicates that that person is deceased also.

- **Death Location:** This is not always entered in an obit, but generally it is.

- **Government Service:** A specialized piece of occupational information that may provide clues for additional research

- **Hobbies**

- **Interment Information:** Name of cemetery. Please note that the name of the cemetery in the obit may be different from where the deceased is actually buried. The burial location could have been changed at the last minute. Or the remains may have been moved to another cemetery later.

- **Maiden Name:** May not be written if the deceased is a married woman. But if the obit names her brothers, their surname may be the surname of the deceased woman at birth

- **Marriage "History" Hints:** Notice a reference to "step-children. That may imply that the deceased had been married before. Helps to clarify whose children were whose.

- **Membership in Lodges, Associations and Clubs**

- **Military Service:** Might be stated, especially if they served in a war. Notice if a flag is on the obit. That denotes a veteran.

- **Mortuary:** This is useful because mortuary records often have much more information than what is written in the obit. So a researcher can contact the mortuary for additional records.

- **Name of Spouse**

- **Names and Residences of Children and Grandchildren:** This is especially helpful when census records are not available. Where else are you going to find children's names?

- **Names of Children and Grandchildrens' Spouses:** This is a recent phenomenon in obituaries, where the name of the spouse of the children/grandchildren is entered. This can help for further cousin finding.

- **Names of Siblings:** Especially helpful if the deceased is a married woman with brothers. See next item

- **Nativity:** Maybe this does not identify the exact place of birth, but at least where the deceased immigrated from.

- **Occupation**

- **Parents and Grandparents Names**

- **Picture of the Deceased**

- **Religion:** Generally indicated by which church/temple is handling the funeral service.

- **Residences:** Generally states the most recent city of residence. Helpful for finding someone in a prior census or city directory. In older obits you may find the language, "Philadelphia and Baltimore papers, please copy." This provides clues as to the deceased's prior residences.

- **Schools Attended**

- **Sports:** What the deceased participated in and who they rooted for

- **Unions:** Did they belong to a union? If so, maybe union records can become an additional set of records to search for additional info.

9 Ways to Effectively Find Obituaries in Online Newspapers

Use Keywords in your search criteria. This will get you directly to the obituary section of the newspaper generally.

- Beloved

- Dear

- Loving

- Passed away

- Survived by

- Died

- Funeral

- In lieu of flowers

- Native of

- Devoted

Continue Searching after finding the first obit.

- Sometimes they are amended after the first publication

Check Papers in places they lived before.

- Obituaries are sometimes copied in other locations

- They might have died far from home, so search both locations

A Death Index is not an Obituary Index.

- Death Indexes do not (usually) have the newspaper title & date.

Use Smart Browse techniques.

- Recognize that the Vital Statistics sections of many old newspapers were on the same page from issue to issue. So, when browsing from day to day after the known death date, just go to the same page number from issue to issue

Use Obituary Indexes from libraries and societies.

- Find your ancestor in these indexes and then (Hopefully if the newspaper title and date are online) go to the issue and then to the Obituary section to get the obit.

Obituaries in the Last 20 Years.

- Can be found generally online, so use your favorite search engine

4. General Advice

If we don't write our ancestors history… who will?

10 Bits of Advice for New Genealogy Researchers

This is going to be a different kind list of items for new (and newish) genealogy researchers and family historians. I am not going to try to suggest how or what to research. There are tons of places for you to find information about researching. Hopefully this list will help you in a different way, because there is so much out there for you to learn from: books, podcasts, blogs, webinars, conferences, etc. And it is easy to get lost, or at least confused. There is also pressure to "do it right" either from others or self-imposed.

At some time in my genealogy learning experience, I have dealt with all of these "do's and don'ts."

- **Do not try to learn "above your head."** I watched a webinar the other day from a well-known genealogist about what should have been a reasonably easy subject to present. In a word, the webinar "sucked." The audience was a mix of mostly beginners and some intermediates. It was presented as if the audience had significant prior knowledge. The presentation was quite confusing – at least to me. I am not a professional expert but have been in this field for over 15 years and can tell a good education piece from a lousy one. So don't try to learn something that you aren't ready for or that is confusing the heck out of you. Turn it off or stop reading and go back to basics.

- **Do not be intimidated by those who seem to be smarter than you.** Not many are smarter than you; they just have more experience and every single one of them started with no knowledge at all – just like you. And since many experts in any field are lousy presenters, it may appear that they are "smarter". A good presenter or writer will care more about the audience than they will about their own ego and will write and speak in a way that is understandable – to you – the viewer/reader. So, gravitate to the educational materials that help you learn – and not confuse you. And find presenters and writers that you truly feel that you can learn from. Ignore the rest at first.

- **Do analyze the heck out of every record or piece of evidence that you have.** Sometimes we get so excited for example, to find a marriage certificate, that we neglect to look at the witnesses mentioned. They may provide important clues. The same is true of obituaries – I always tell people to carefully analyze every single word in the obit. Believe me, there is stuff hidden in these newspaper articles that could help you fill out the branch of the tree that the deceased belongs to.

- **Do not be intimidated by the "cite your source rules."** Writing down where you found stuff is very important, for no other reason than you will want to know where you found it when you are analyzing the information later. There are guidelines that have been written that are excellent but may seem a bit intimidating. Try your best to follow them and give yourself time to apply them. You will get it eventually. Be patient with yourself.

- **Do take a genealogy "break" occasionally.** Sometimes we get stuck on one branch of our tree, or a so called "brick wall." Take a break and work on photos or stories or some other branch that might be a little easier. Or better yet, take a week or so where you don't touch your genealogy project. That might refresh your mind for when you get back to it.

- **Do make realistic goals.** And don't get caught up in the "numbers game." Some people like to brag that they have 15,000 people in their family tree, or that they can trace back to the 12th century. I mean – Really? I frankly don't care about these sometimes ego-driven statements. In my opinion, having a well-evidenced tree where you also know something about the inhabitants of the tree, as well as being pretty darn sure that the tree is "correct" should be the goal.

- **Do get out of the house.** All records that you are seeking are not available online. That is a fact and will be a fact (in my opinion) likely almost forever. Remember it costs money to digitize all this stuff. Subscription sites have a financial incentive to digitize records. Libraries and historical societies who own record collections on paper have to obtain funding and donations to get the money to microfilm and/or digitize their records. And as terrific as FamilySearch is to do the digitization that they do, they are not going to be able to digitize everything either. With this in mind, you need to get out and visit libraries, genealogy societies, courthouses, and archives to get access to these non-digitized records. Besides, it's fun. A few years ago, I had a great time finding out about my great great grandfather in a very small library in California. They had records from a lodge that he belonged to in the 1850s. Trust me – those handwritten records would be near the bottom of a list of items to ever be digitized.

- **Don't just focus on dates.** Yes, birth, marriage, and death date information is important to make sure you have the correct people in your family tree. But also focus on their life stories by searching newspapers for interesting articles and anecdotes about their lives. And spend some time with photograph identification with your known relatives and those new "cousins" that you find via your research. That is great fun.

And most importantly:

Don't let anyone or any challenge diminish your enthusiasm. And don't lose your curiosity.

Do have fun. For 99% of the people in the world who are searching for their ancestors and their stories, it is a hobby. Hobbies are supposed to be fun. Remember that.

Two Hidden Secrets for the FamilySearch Catalog

Here are two hidden secrets to find a ton more results from the FamilySearch catalog. Full disclosure: I love the FamilySearch (FS) Catalog! For those collections that are available online, and the books that have been digitized, there are hundreds of thousands to choose from. For the online collections and books, I can use my PC at home to scroll through digitized page after digitized page, just as if I had my own microfilm reader, only without the hassle. But there are a couple of hidden secrets that you need to know if you wish to maximize your results. And they are not easy to discover, which is why I am relating them to you now.

Secret #1: Use Keyword Searches

The first secret relates to searching through the catalog for records. Let's first look at the catalog's search function.

What I want to find are **Funeral Home records from Los Angeles County**, California that are available only online. I am not interested in knowing where the microfilm is located or those that are only available at a Family History Center (FHC).

The logical place to start is to enter the place for which the collections have been digitized by clicking on [Place] in the top menu.

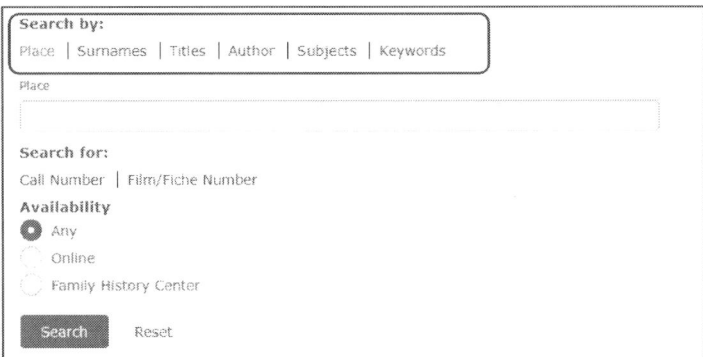

The first screen is where I enter the **Place**, and the online catalog will show me which collections are available. For entering the place, I click in that [Place] textbox, enter "Los Angeles," and then select from the pop-up menu, "United States, California, Los Angeles", which signifies Los Angeles County.

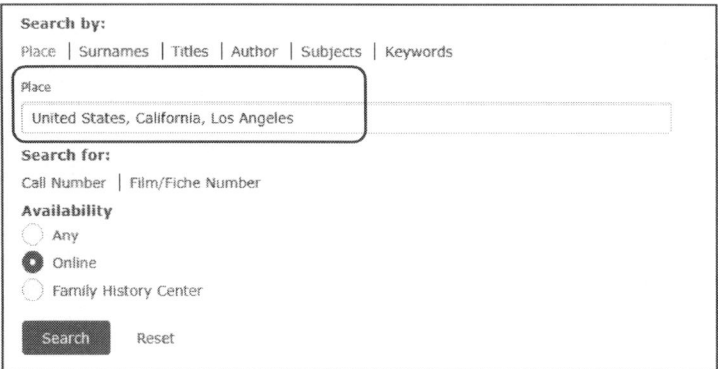

Here is the screen of results after entering the Place and clicking the [Search] button.

As you can see, it presents me with one Funeral Home collection. Only one. This is what is presented to me when I click on that line - a collection for Pierce Brothers Mortuary.

> ▼ **United States, California, Los Angeles - Funeral homes (1)**
>
> Funeral records, 1958-1990
>
> Author: Pierce Brothers Mortuary (Los Angeles, California)

Now for the secret trick that will optimize the number of collections returned to you. This time I am going to go back to the main search screen and click on [Keywords] in the top menu, ignoring the Place for now.

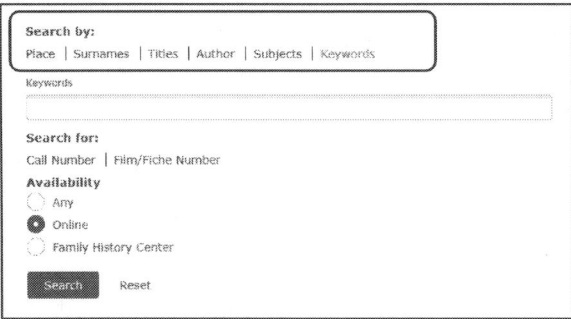

On this screen, I make sure that the [Online] availability option is selected, I enter "los angeles funeral home" in the [Keyword] textbox, and click the [Search] button.

Holy mackerel! Now there are 30 online funeral home collections for Los Angeles County. The one we found in the very first search appears as the fifth hit in the second search using just keywords. So, entering the place in the Place box doesn't retrieve the optimal number of collections.

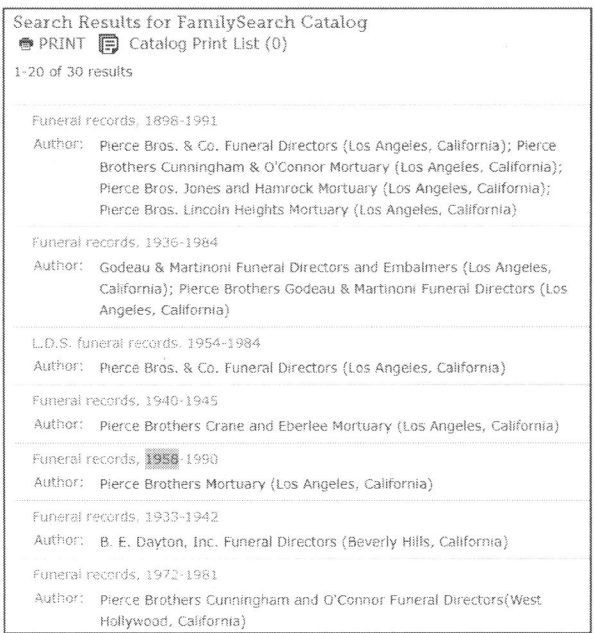

Secret #1 Summary: Always use keyword searching when looking for online collections from the FamilySearch Catalog, and make sure that you select the [Online] option before clicking on [Search]. You will receive far more pertinent results.

Secret #2: Stay Logged In

- When searching in FamilySearch, however you are doing it, you need to first have a free account and be logged in (or signed in). It is really easy to sign up.

- But here is the kicker: FamilySearch logs me out all the time when I am using the site, unbeknownst to me. I am going to show you the results of a FamilySearch Catalog search, and one of the collections that is in the results list.

- The first image example is when I am logged in, and the second image example when I have been logged out, and I will show you the differences.

- The differences are stark when you are looking for online collections, which I will discuss.

These images are smaller, to fit on this page. They look exactly the same, right?

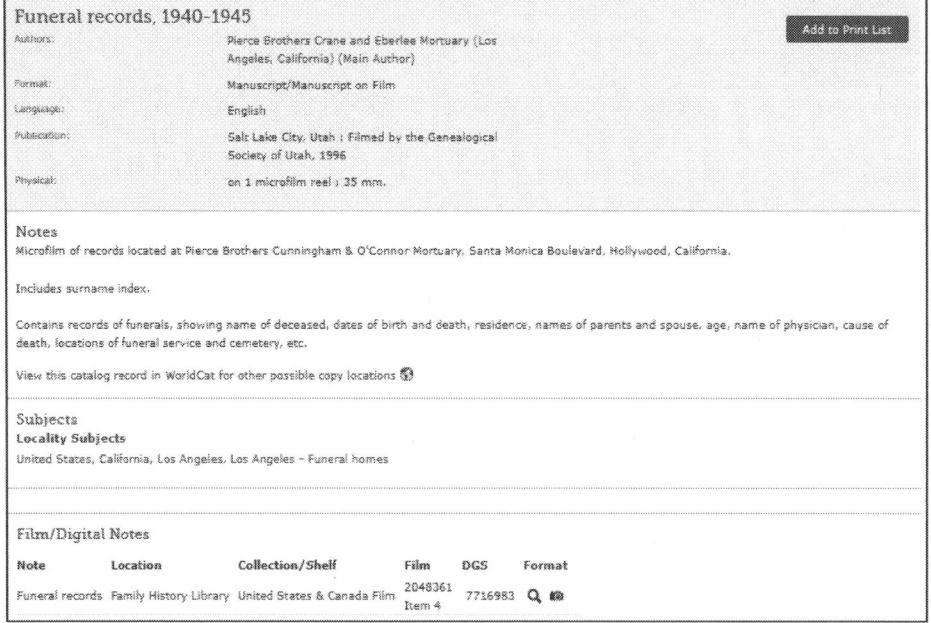

Nope. See at the bottom under "Format"? The logged in image has a camera icon, and the logged-out image has a camera with a key.

What's the difference, you ask? Near the bottom of each collection page under Film/Digital Notes is the name of each sub-collection. If there is a camera icon at the right of the name (in the Format column) then the collections' images are browsable online. If there is a camera with a key icon, it is only available at a Family History Center or affiliated library. If there is a film reel icon, then it is only available in microfilm format, not digital. Finally, if there is a magnifying glass icon, the collection is searchable.

Secret #2 Summary: Always stay logged in. And regularly check if you are on the site for a long time because FamilySearch will log you out regularly if you are on a long time, and you won't even know it unless you look at the top right of each page where it tells you if you are signed in or not.

FamilySearch Summary: The Moral of the Story is easy to remember: When searching the FS Catalog, 1) always use keyword searches and 2) always stay signed in. That's all there is to optimizing your results that you can browse through - online - at home - in your PJs if you are so inclined!

17 Tips for Using Google for Genealogy Research

Normally when people think of Google, they think of the search engine. As genealogy researchers, it is imperative that we learn to use the Google search engine effectively, since it can helps us find ancestors, relevant documents, and many more pertinent things to help find our ancestors.

Using the Google Search Engine
Effectively for Genealogy Research

- A basic search in Google requires us to enter search criteria in the Search box. This can be something simple such as a full name or surname. Or a much more complicated entry. When using multiple words in the criteria it is assumed to be a **Boolean AND**. For example, Word1 Word2 Word3 as your search criteria means that all three words must appear to provide a positive search result or rank highest in the list of results.

- If you are searching for a **multi-word phrase** that must appear as the phrase, simply, put double quotes before and after the phrase.
  For example, "Word1 Word2 Word3"

- If you wish to **exclude a word** from your search, simply include a minus sign (hyphen) before the word that you wish to exclude.
  For example, John Dulles –Foster

- Want to include **synonyms** in your search? Just place a tilde symbol in front of the word that you are looking for a synonym.
  For example Word1 ~Word2

- To search within a **specific site**, enter the word site: in front of the URL of the site.
  For example site:youtube.com

- To **exclude results from a specific site** because you have already searched it or it dominates the results and you don't wish to see results from that site, just put a minus sign (hyphen) in front of the site term. In our previous example where you want to exclude results from YouTube, just enter –site:youtube.com

- Use the **OR operator** if you wish to include multiple words or phrases in a search.
  For example Lincoln OR "Emancipation Proclamation"

- Although Google's searches with multiple words assume an AND operation, you can use the AND operator. This is useful when you have a more complicated criteria that has a **combination of OR and AND operations** in your search criteria.

- **Wildcard searches** can be performed by entering an asterisk (*) in your search criteria.

- To return a **prior version** of a web page enter cache:xyz.com. It is different from the Internet Archive's Wayback Machine. Google presents just the most recent version of a web page, whereas the Wayback Machine presents multiple versions.

- To restrict results to specific **file types**, enter your criteria as follows: searchword filetype pdf

- To find results from **related websites** enter related:website1.com

- To find results for a search for a word **within the title**, enter intitle:cemetery

- To find results for **multiple words** that appear **within the title**, enter allintitle:cemetery burial

- To find results for a word (or text string) that appears **in a URL**, enter allinurl:textstring

- To perform a **proximity search**, i.e. finding words within a specified number of words from one another, use the AROUND function.
  For example, Word1 AROUND(5) Word2 finds occurrences where Word1 is within 5 words from Word2.

Beyond the Search Engine: Using Google Databases

Google has a number of databases and functions that we can search and use, such as Google Books, Google Scholar, and others that are useful to us as genealogy researchers. Here is an overview of some of these databases and functions.

- **Google Books** has a seemingly never-ending supply of digitized books. And there is an ample number of old books that can be used in your genealogy research. Generally, there are two types of entries: books that are digitized and full text of the entire book is available online, and books where only partial sections or pages are available, and only snippets of your resultant search results provide useful information. The URL is https://books.google.com.

- **Google Patents** presents a search engine to find old patents from around the world. Personally, I found that five of my ancestors held patents, much to my surprise, and several of them were from the 1800s! The URL is https://patents.google.com.

- **Google Cache** provides the ability to see a previous version of a web page. This is particularly useful when you get a 404 Error and/or a "File Not Found" page when going to a website. Just enter "cache:" in front (do not enter the quotes) of the desired webpages URL, and it will take you to the previous version.

- **Google News Archive** unfortunately is no longer adding new titles to its collection, but it still is searchable. You can see the list of over 1,400 titles and search the collection at this URL: https://news.google.com/newspapers?hl=en.

- **Google Scholar** (from Google): provides a simple way to broadly search for scholarly literature. From one place, you can search across many disciplines and sources: articles, theses, books, abstracts, and court opinions from academic publishers, professional societies, online repositories, universities, and other web sites. The URL is https://scholar.google.com.

- **Google Images** has over 28 Billion images in its database. Similar search functions as in generic Google Search are available. There also is a reverse image search. This is particularly useful for genealogists as it may find other researchers who have the same or similar photo as that of your ancestor that you are performing the reverse image search for or even an image base somewhere with pertinent photos. The URL is https://www.google.com/imghp?hl=en.

- **Google Maps and Google Earth** are particularly useful for genealogists as we can see visually what a house, business, or other property looks like. Also creating custom maps of our ancestors' residences can also provide us with genealogical clues. The URLs are https://www.google.com/maps and https://earth.google.com/web.

- **Google Translate** is very useful when attempting to convert written documents, letters, or other material from the language of the "old country" to current language. There are over 100 languages available. The URL is https://translate.google.com.

- **Google Alerts** is an excellent resource for genealogy researchers. It is like having a constant search running all the time. It won't necessarily search inside databases or their records, but if a mention of a person, surname, or whatever else you set the Alert up for occurs, you will be sent an email. It can be your secret weapon! The URL is https://www.google.com/alerts.

Notes

5. Immigration, Naturalization, and Travel

Finding that your ancestor immigrated is one thing, but to complete the story, why did they immigrate?

19 Reasons to Research Passport Applications

One of the often-overlooked genealogical documents, are passport applications and the passports themselves. For United States passport applications, required reading is from the U.S. National Archives – Passport Applications (Archives.gov/research/passport). The history, types, limitations, and how to access the microfilms of registers and indexes are included.

So, what unique and interesting information can be found in a U.S. passport application from the collection of 1795 to 1925?

- **Birth date or age**

- **Birthplace**

- **Current residence and length of residency**

- **Date of application or issuance of passport**

- **Date of immigration**

- **Date of naturalization and where and what court**

- **Destination and reason for travel**

- **Father's or husband's birth date or age**

- **Father's or husband's birthplace**

- **Father's or husband's name**

- **Father's or husband's residence**

- **Marital status**

- **Name of applicant**

- **Occupation**

- **Photograph:** This is a huge bonus as these applications provided the only photograph that I have of some ancestors. Low quality, but better than nothing.

- **Physical description:** With no photograph, this may be the only hint of what they looked like.

- **Possible information about children and other relatives**

- **Ship information**

- **Wife's name**

In microfilm form, these are available from National Archives and Records Administration (NARA) and the Family History Library in Salt Lake City.

Online, check out these collections.

FamilySearch.org: Free to Public

- United States Passport Applications, 1795-1925

  https://www.FamilySearch.org/search/collection/2185145?collection NameFilter=false

- Hawaii, Passport Records, 1874-1898

  https://www.FamilySearch.org/search/collection/3021682

- Passport Documents from Fiji, Finland, Germany, Portugal, and Spain

  https://www.FamilySearch.org/search/collection/list/?cqs=passport

Ancestry.com: Subscription Required

- U.S. Passport Applications, 1795-1925

  https://search.ancestry.com/search/db.aspx?dbid=1174

- Connecticut, Passport and Birth Certificates, 1852-1928

  https://search.ancestry.com/search/db.aspx?dbid=2276

- U.S. Consular Posts, Emergency Passport Applications, 1915-1926

  https://search.ancestry.com/search/db.aspx?dbid=1505

- Hawaii, Passport Records, 1849-1850, 1874-1900

  https://search.ancestry.com/search/db.aspx?dbid=61076

- Passport Documents from Belarus, Latvia, Lithuania, France, Portugal, and Romania

    https://www.ancestry.com/search/collections/catalog/?keyword=passport

FindMyPast.com: Subscription Required

- United States Passport Applications

    https://search.findmypast.com/search-world-Records/united-states-passport-applications

Fold3.com: Subscription Required

- Passport Applications, 1795-1905

    https://www.fold3.com/search/#query=passport&offset=14&t=447

MyHeritage.com: Free to Public

- United States Passport Applications, 1795-1925

    https://www.myheritage.com/research/collection-10720/united-states-passport-applications-1795-1925

20 Reasons to Use Naturalization Records

Do you research naturalization records? No? Why not? Does the thought of going through paper files in dusty court basements turn you off? Well – I'm here to tell you that it is worth it – and with recent digitization efforts – more and more original documents have been scanned and been made available via microfilm or even online.

Some of the larger subscription sites have made some source documents available – as well as index cards that can lead you to the court that handled the proceedings.

Whatever! It is worth the effort – no matter what. The amount of information on naturalization records is in a word – Outstanding! Take a look below at the 20 or so types of information that can be found.

Post-1906 there are four awesome documents that just drip with great information:

- Declaration of Intent

- Petition for Citizenship or Naturalization

- Certificate of Arrival

- Certificate of Naturalization

Many of the online genealogy websites may not have all these documents available, but do have index cards that are searchable, which has information regarding the court handling the proceedings. With this information you might be able to track down some of the source documents. So, lets' go; what types of information are included in these documents?

- **Age**

- **Birth Date**

- **Birth Location**

- **Children:** Names, place of birth and current residence

- **Current Address**

- **Emigration Information:** Port of departure, name of ship/vessel, and date of departure

- **Former Names:** If they changed their name or if they got married in the U.S. may provide great clues for additional research, especially in their birth country or former country of residence

- **Immigration Information:** Port of arrival and date of arrival

- **Last Foreign Residence**

- **Marital Status**

- **Marriage Date**

- **Marriage Location**

- **Name and Location** of court handling the proceedings

- **Name:** (often includes middle name which is useful). Can help with spelling of more complex names for future searching as well.

- **Occupation**

- **Photo**

- **Physical Characteristics:** Color/race, complexion, height and weight, hair and eye color, and scars or other distinctive marks.

- **Signature:** Always fun to see how they signed their name

- **Spouse Information:** Name of spouse and their birth location and current address. Also, when they entered the U.S. May include their naturalization information if applicable

- **Witnesses:** Names, occupations, and addresses – always useful (and underappreciated), may provide means of alternative research if the same surname – or if a friend – possible clues

45 Reasons to Research Immigration Records

When I first started my ancestor research, after I had gotten over the initial excitement of reviewing census records and interviewing my living relatives, I almost immediately began trying to find my immigrant ancestors and how they got to America. Through free repositories such as Ellis Island and Castle Garden and other sites, as well as records available via subscription sites, I plugged away.

After collecting a few records, I began to analyze the contents of those records. There are tons of information included in them, and thorough analysis can lead you to discover familial relationships that are much beyond what ship they arrived in and on what date they immigrated. My first few records were from the mid-1850s and all that was on the passenger lists were name, age, sex, occupation, and where they were coming from. Make sure that you analyze the hospital/medical detainment information for the trip also. Later lists have much more information requested and on the passenger lists, as you can see below.

- **Ability to Read and/or Write:** Also indicates which language they were proficient in

- **Age**

- **Anarchist?**

- **Been to the U.S. Before?**

- **Complexion Type**

- **Date of Arrival**

- **Date of Departure**

- **Deformed or Crippled?**

- **Detained Aliens:** Date of Discharge

- **Detained Aliens:** Final Disposition

- **Detained Aliens:** Name

- **Detained Aliens:** Number of Meals Provided

- **Detained Aliens:** Reason for Detention – usually medical; the form is not shown here but is a separate form

- **Do You Have a Ticket for Final Destination?**

- **Ever Been in Prison, Almshouse, Mental Institution or Supported by Charity?**

- **Ever Excluded from U.S., Deported or Arrested?**

- **Eye Color**

- **Family:** Families certainly did travel together and sometimes not, and sometimes not on the same ship or in the same year. Other relatives may have been on the same ship, so look at all the manifest pages. Just like in census records, a page or two away may be an aunt, a cousin, or another relative.

- **Final Destination:** City/Town and State

- **For Aircraft:** Carrier and Flight Number

- **Gender**

- **Hair Color**

- **Height:** Just one of the physical characteristics requested in the form. In lieu of a lack of a photo for an ancestor – these characteristics provide some clue as to what they looked like.

- **How Much Money in Your Possession?**

- **Labor Contract?**

- **Length of Intended Stay**

- **Marital Status**

- **Marks of Identification**

- **Name and Address of Contact for Location from Whence they Came:** This is very useful information because it may provide information about a family member in the "old country" that you may know nothing about

- **Name of Ship**

- **Name of the Immigrant:** Despite the legend that names were changed at Ellis Island, they certainly were not. But folks did change their name later. Members of my own family changed their Hebrew names to their English/American equivalents – not necessarily at the time of immigration but at some point later. So, searching for the Anglicized name may not bear fruit in these cases when searching for their immigration records.

- **Nationality or Citizenship**

- **Occupation**

- **Part of the Vessel for Travel:** Which deck, for example

- **Physical and Mental Health Condition?**

- **Place of Birth:** City/town and country

- **Place of Last Residence:** City/town and country

- **Polygamist?**

- **Port/City of Arrival**

- **Port/City of Departure**

- **Purpose for Coming to the U.S.**

- **Race**

- **Visa:** Number and where and when issued

- **Whether Going to Visit a Relative or Friend:** Name and complete address is requested in this entry. Similar to the contact person from whence they came, this entry can also provide terrific clues as to other relatives of the immigrant.

- **Who Paid for Your Passage?**

Historical Naturalization and Immigration Laws

The following are from 1790 through 1952.

- **1790:** Naturalization Act of 1790 – Two years residency; restricted to "free white persons" of "good moral character"

- **1795:** Naturalization Act of 1795 – Five years residency plus three years notice of intent to apply for citizenship

- **1798:** Naturalization Act of 1798 – 14 years residency and five years notice of intent to apply for citizenship

- **1802:** Repealed and replaced the 1798 act; Five years residency and three years notice of intent to apply for citizenship. Resident children of naturalized citizens are considered citizens; children born abroad of US citizens are considered citizens

- **1824:** Reduced time from notice of intent to citizenship to 2 years. 5 years residency still required.

- **1855:** Women take on the citizenship of her husband through derivative citizenship.

- **1866:** Civil Rights Act of 1866 provide that "All persons born in the US and not subject to any foreign power, excluding Indians not taxed, are citizens, and such citizens of every race and color without regard to any previous condition of slavery or in servitude shall have the same rights as enjoyed by white citizens".

- **1868:** 14th Amendment reads "All persons born or naturalized in the US, and subject to the jurisdiction thereof, are citizens of the US"

- **1870:** Law expanded to allow African blacks to be naturalized; Asians could immigrate but could not be naturalized

- **1875:** Page Act barred immigrants considered "undesirable," defining this as a person from East Asia who was coming to the United States to be a forced laborer, any East Asian woman who would engage in prostitution, and all people considered to be convicts in their own country

- **1882:** The Chinese Exclusion Act limited further Chinese immigration. The law was later changed and repealed. Did not deal with naturalization issues.

- **1891:** Expanded the list of exclusions for immigration from prior laws to include those who have a contagious disease and polygamists.

- **1903:** Banned anarchists, beggars, and importers of prostitutes from immigrating.

- **1907:** A Gentlemen's Agreement stopped Japan from issuing visas, but many Japanese immigrants immigrated through Hawaii.

- **1907:** Under the act of March 2, 1907, all women acquired their husband's nationality upon a marriage that occurred after that date. However, U.S.-born citizen women could now lose their citizenship by any marriage to any alien.

- **1922:** The Cable Act provided that a woman had a nationality of her own. No marriage since that date has granted U.S. citizenship to any alien woman nor taken it from any U.S.-born women who married an alien eligible to naturalization. Under the new law women became eligible to naturalize nearly on the same terms as men. A difference was for those women whose husbands had already naturalized. If her husband was a citizen, the wife did not need to file a declaration of intention. She could initiate naturalization proceedings with a petition alone.

- **1936:** Women who were native born citizens and lost citizenship because of marriage prior to September 22, 1922, are considered a citizen if she took the oath of allegiance and her marriage was terminated by either death or divorce.

- **1940:** In 1940 Congress allowed all women who lost citizenship by marriage between 1907 and 1922 to repatriate, or resume their citizenship, regardless of their marital status. Since then, any woman who lost U.S. citizenship in those years by marriage to an alien, could resume her citizenship by applying and taking the oath of allegiance.

- **1952:** Declaration of Intent no longer required; five years residency still required.

6. Military

Did your ancestor serve in a war?
What did that do to color their life?

28 Things You Can Find in Military Records

Military records are yet another very useful set of records that will help you in finding more about your ancestors. There are a ton of records that are available for free online, and there are some very robust subscription-only collections (such as Fold3 and Ancestry) that have sizable online military collections as well.

Typically, military records online fall into 5 different categories. The specific information that you should be targeting in your research is listed for each category:

Military Service Records

- Birth date and location

- Contact information of next of kin

- Date enlisted, mustered out

- Full name

- Location of enlistment

- Medical and military information

- Occupation

- Rank

- Residence

- Unit assignations while in the military

Selective Service Records

- Age

- Birthplace

- Contact information

- Employer

- Full name

- Marital status

- Occupation

- Physical description

- Residence

Bounty Land Warrant Applications

- Includes similar information as in service records as well as other information, such as number of warrants, date of issuance, and number of acres. Only used between 1775 and 1855.

Pension Records

- Birth, Marriage and Death information (dates and locations)

- Demographic information

- Information about the spouse and children

- Pension balance

- Rank and Unit

Special Records

- 1910-1940 Census Records include questions about military service

- Information if the person was a prisoner of war, wounded or killed in action, or MIA

- Veteran's cemeteries burial lists

Historical U.S. Draft Registration and Enrollment

- **Pre-1861:** No federal system, state militias, most with different rules

- **1863:** Enrollment Act of 1863; involuntarily called men to service

- **1917:** May 18; Selective Service Act of 1917 passed by Congress

- **1917:** 1st registration, June 5; men aged 21 to 31

- **1918:** 2nd registration, June 5; men turning 21 after 1st registration; supplemental on August 24 for men turning 21 after June 5

- **1918:** 3rd registration, September 12; all men aged 18 to 45

- **1940:** September 16; President Roosevelt signs peacetime Selective Service Act

- **1940:** 1st registration, October 16; For men born between 17 October 1904 and 16 October 1919 (ages 21-35) living within the continental United States.

- **1940:** Initial draft, October 29; A man had to be between 21 and 45, at least 5' tall and no taller than 6'6", weigh at least 105 lbs., have vision correctable with glasses, and have at least half his teeth. He had to be able to read and write, and not have been convicted of a crime.

- **1941:** 2nd registration, July 1; For men born between 17 October 1919 and 12 July 1920 who had turned 21 since the first registration & men from the first draft who did not register. The prefix "S" preceded the serial #.

- **1942:** 3rd registration, February 16; For men born between 17 February 1897 and 31 December 1921 (ages 20-45) who had not previously registered. The prefix "T" preceded the serial #.

- **1942:** 4th registration, April 27 (Old Man's Draft); born between 27 April 1877 and 16 February 1890. The prefix "U" preceded the serial number.

- **1942:** 5th registration, June 30; For men born between 1 January 1922 and 30 June 1924 (ages 18-20). The prefix "N" preceded the serial #.

- **1942:** 6th registration, December 10-31; For men born between 1 July and 31 December 1924 (men who had turned 18 after 12 November 1942.) The prefix "W" preceded the serial #.

- **1943:** Additional registration, November 16-December 31; For American citizens living abroad between the ages of 18 and 45.

- **1947-49:** Men aged 18 to 26 were required to register.

- **1950-53:** Men aged 18 to 26 were required to register. Deferments were available for students, some fathers, farmers, and other occupations which supported the national interest.

- **1953-71:** Men aged 18 to 26 were required to register. Student, fatherhood, occupational and agricultural deferments

- **1970:** Vietnam Lottery, December 1, 1969; applied to year of birth 1944-50

- **1971:** Vietnam Lottery, July 1, 1970; applied to year of birth 1951

- **1971:** Deferments were phased out.

- **1972:** Vietnam Lottery, August 5, 1971; applied to year of birth 1952

- **1973:** Vietnam Lottery, February 2, 1972; applied to year of birth 1953

- **1974:** Vietnam Lottery, March 8, 1973; applied to year of birth 1954

- **1975:** Vietnam Lottery, March 20, 1974; applied to year of birth 1955

- **1976:** Vietnam Lottery, March 12, 1975; applied to year of birth 1956

- **1975:** Registration was suspended April 1, 1975, by Presidential Proclamation

- **1980:** Men are required to register with the Selective Service System within 30 days of their 18th birthday

Notes

7. Miscellaneous

Finding out that one of our ancestors was a murderer, a
philanderer, or a robber is no reason to smile…
unless you are a family historian.

20 Things You Can Find in Church Records

Prior to the recording of civil records and even now, Church Records have become a necessary, and valuable category of collections that should be researched. They provide information that often cannot be found anywhere else. Baptisms, marriages, and funerals are commonly thought of when we discuss church records, but there is so much more. For example, I found the death date of one of my relatives in Berlin, Germany via a Church Newsletter!

Here is a list of the valuable information contained in Church Records and why you should be researching them:

- **Admissions of New Members:** These will be recorded in the membership list and/or church newsletter. The date of entry may indicate when someone moved to a new location.

- **Baptisms and Christenings:** Names of godparents and witnesses are often included as well as the names of the child and parents. Parish where the family is residing, legitimacy of the child, etc. These additional names may provide relationship clues.

- **Burials:** If it is a church-affiliated cemetery, the burial information will be recorded in the church's records.

- **Church Cemetery Records:** Includes name of deceased, date of death, burial date, and place, sometimes age and cause of death.

- **Church Directories:** Like membership lists, these might include residence information and other contact information of the church clergy and all members.

- **Church Minutes:** The church officials often would conduct meetings to discuss the administrative and business side of the church, and the meetings would be recorded in official minutes of the meetings

- **Church Newsletters:** Regularly published documents that discuss events of the church, new members, transferring members, birthdays, anniversaries, births, marriages, and deaths of members

- **Church Newspapers and Magazines:** A more recent phenomenon; essentially another way, like a newsletter, to communicate between the church and congregants and members

- **Clergy Admissions and Dismissals:** Might be included in the church minutes; also, may be formal documents from the higher ups in the church organizational structure for a larger area

- **Confirmations, Bar/Bat Mitzvahs:** These are generally recorded by the church or synagogue.

- **Deaths and Funerals:** If the funeral "ceremony" is conducted in a church, it is generally recorded.

- **Disciplinary Actions Against Members:** Might be recorded in the Church Minutes

- **Dismissals:** For whatever reason, an individual or family may be dismissed from the church. These would be recorded.

- **Family Relationships:** May be specifically documented in membership lists, or can be determined from people attending baptisms, weddings, or funerals.

- **Letters of Introduction:** A current church official might write to assist the member and family in joining a new church within the denomination, but in a different area.

- **Marriages:** Church weddings are documented. In more modern times, witnesses are required in order to civilly record the marriage and may be required in some religions.

- **Membership Lists:** Members and congregants are kept in membership lists. These are quite useful to compare year to year, as an absence from the list may indicate that a member may have moved their residence, passed on, or joined another church.

- **Newspaper Obituaries and Other Articles:** Clues to church membership can be found in historical newspaper articles such as obituaries. Also, upcoming, and past church events will be documented in newspapers.

- **Sunday School Lists:** Lists of children who attend Sunday School, as well as the teacher's name.

- **Transfers of Memberships Out of the Church:** There even may be a formal document indicating that the member leaves in good standing with the church.

40 Old Time Illnesses and Their Current Names

- **Ablepsy:** Blindness

- **Ague:** Flu-like symptoms likely caused by malaria

- **Apoplexy:** Stroke

- **Barrel fever:** Alcoholism

- **Biliousness:** Jaundice

- **Black dog:** Depression

- **Blood Poisoning:** Sepsis or septicemia

- **Breakbone:** Dengue fever

- **Bronze John:** Yellow fever

- **Camp Fever:** Typhus

- **Chalkstones:** Swelling with pain that probably was caused by rheumatoid arthritis or gout

- **Congestive Fever:** Malaria

- **Consumption:** Tuberculosis

- **Domestic Malady:** Depression or another sort of emotional breakdown

- **Dropsy:** Swelling caused by fluid retention

- **Dropsy of the Brain:** Encephalitis

- **Double Personality:** Manic depressive

- **Falling Sickness:** Epilepsy

- **French Pox:** Syphilis

- **Frigid:** Low sex drive

- **Green Sickness or Green Fever:** Anemia

- **Grip, Gripe or Grippe:** Flu

- **Idiot Savant:** Developmentally delayed and exceptionally talented

- **Jail Fever:** Typhus

- **Leprosy:** Hansen's disease

- **Lumbago:** Back pain

- **Mad Cow:** Creutzfeldt-Jakob disease

- **Melancholia:** Severe depression

- **Mortification:** Gangrene

- **Palsy:** Problems with muscle control, such as tremors or paralysis

- **Quincy or Quinsy:** Tonsillitis

- **Retarded:** Developmentally or cognitively delayed

- **Scrumpox:** Impetigo

- **Ship Fever:** Typhus

- **St Vitus Dance:** Chorea.

- **Swine Flu:** H1N1 virus

- **Change of Life:** Menopause

- **The Shakes:** Parkinson's disease

- **Winter Fever:** Pneumonia

- **Went Under:** Had anesthesia

Was Your Ancestor in a Lodge, Club, or Secret Society?

Why is this important? 20 to 40% of men in 1900 are estimated to have belonged to a lodge or club; their membership was often cited in Obituaries. Here are a few of the more prominent ones.

- **B'nai B'rith:** A Jewish service organization.

- **Benevolent and Protective Order of Elks:** A fraternal order focused on charity, justice, brotherly love, and fidelity with an emphasis on patriotism and belief in God.

- **Colonial Dames of America:** An American organization composed of women who are descended from an ancestor who lived in British America from 1607–1775.

- **Daughters of Norway:** A sisterhood aimed at preserving Nordic heritage.

- **Daughters of the American Revolution (DAR):** A lineage-based membership service organization for women who are directly descended from a person involved in the United States' efforts towards independence.

- **Fraternal Order of Eagles:** "People Helping People" in the spirit of liberty, truth, justice, and equality. Local units are called "Aeries."

- **Freemasons:** The Masonic Fraternity claims to be the oldest Fraternity in the world and seeks men (Masons) wishing to become better men through service and self-improvement.

- **Grange:** A community-based, fraternal organization with an interest in representing rural residents and the agriculture community.

- **Independent Order of Odd Fellows:** To improve and elevate the character of mankind by promoting the principles of friendship, love, truth, faith, hope, charity, and universal justice.

- **International Concatenated Order of Hoo-Hoo, Incorporated:** A fraternal and service organization whose members are involved in the forests products industry.

- **Job's Daughters International:** A Masonic affiliated youth organization for girls and young women aged 10 to 20.

- **Kiwanis:** An international service club founded in 1915 in Detroit, Michigan.

- **Knight of Pythias:** A fraternal organization and secret society founded in Washington, D.C., in February 1864.

- **Knights of Columbus:** A Catholic fraternal benefit society.

- **Lions Club:** An international non-political service organization established originally in 1917 in Chicago, Illinois.

- **Loyal Order of Moose:** A fraternal and service organization founded in 1888 and headquartered in Mooseheart, Illinois.

- **Optimist International:** An international service club organization with almost 3,000 clubs and over 80,000 members in more than 20 countries. The international headquarters is located in St. Louis, Missouri.

- **Order of the Eastern Star:** The members of the Order of the Eastern Star are dedicated women and men who sincerely reflect the spirit of fraternal love and the desire to work together for good.

- **Rebekahs:** This is the female organization of the Independent Order of Odd Fellows

- **Rotary International:** An international service organization whose stated purpose is to bring together business and professional leaders to provide humanitarian service and to advance goodwill and peace around the world.

- **Shriners:** Fraternity based on fun, fellowship and the Masonic principles of brotherly love, relief, and truth.

- **Sons of Italy:** A fraternal group focused on preserving Italian heritage.

- **Sons of Norway:** A fraternal group focused on preserving Norwegian heritage. Founded in 1895.

- **Soroptimist International (SI):** A worldwide volunteer service organization for women who work for peace, and in particular to improve the lives of women and girls.

- **The American Legion:** Commonly known as the Legion, is a nonprofit organization of U.S. war veterans.

9 Reasons Why You Should Be Researching Voter Records

Voter registration records are available online and offline from all over the world and are what I consider a hidden gem of information to assist you in advancing your family history and genealogy research. Here are nine ways that voter records can help you to find more about your ancestors.

- **Fill Gaps between Censuses:** In the ten years between censuses, people move, they die, they get married, etc. The advantage of voter registration records is that they can tell you their address, their occupation, and more. These are generally published annually.

- **Middle Names:** Often a complete name is included in voter registration records; in fact, the only place that I ever found my great grandfather's middle name was in several of these records. Prior to finding them, I only knew his middle name as an initial.

- **Find a Spouse:** After 1920 for all of America, women could vote. So, at that time their names began to show up in Voter Registration records. Some states had passed women's suffrage laws prior to 1920, but just a few. To be complete, women in some states in the late 1700s had voting rights until they were all taken away by 1807. The given name of a woman is sometimes included in the voter registration record. For example, a Mary Smith who was married to a James Smith would be entered as Mrs. Mary Smith. If they both lived at the same address on the registration list, one could surmise that they were married to each other, and you then could certainly search for better evidence; or they could be siblings or have a parent-child relationship. But at least there is a good possibility that they may indeed be married to each other.

- **Naturalization Information:** In some records from the 1800s, the date and place of naturalization is included, which can provide leads for obtaining their detailed naturalization records.

- **Nativity:** In the 1800s, the place of birth is entered, which is especially helpful for naturalized immigrants.

- **Physical Characteristics:** California Great Registers were quite thorough and included age, height, complexion, eye, and hair color, as well as any distinguishing marks or scars.

- **Political Party or Affiliation:** Usually abbreviated as Dem or Rep, but you will find other party names as well, in addition to "None." Remember that Democrats and Republicans from years ago did not necessarily align with the same principles or policies as these political parties do today.

- **Precinct Captains and Election Workers:** Not available in voter registration records, but these are certainly voting related. Look in newspapers and you will find many lists of election workers. Many of my ancestors worked in precincts to assist in the electoral process.

- **Migration:** A few voter registration record sets include a question regarding how long the voter lived in the state, the county, and the precinct. This can be useful to determine when they moved, which can lead to additional research as to their whereabouts for census research—as an example.

Notes

8. Newspaper Research

Historical community newspapers
were the Social Media of their time.

Hidden Gems in Old Newspapers that Amplify Life Stories

If you are trying to add to your ancestor's life stories, what better way than interesting newspaper articles about their lives? Absent direct accounts from your living relatives, seeking these hidden gems in old newspapers will tell you things about your ancestors that there is no other way, absent a biography or autobiographical book, that you would ever know these tidbits.

- **Advertisements:** You never know what you will find in advertisements. In one interesting ad, my great grandfather was a spokesman for some miracle digestive malady cure. And the bonus was that there was a photo of him. (By the way the miracle cure didn't work; he died of stomach issues two years after the advertisement was published). I also saw many ads from my 3rd Great Uncle, who had created a special sauce for food, and created and published ads to sell it.

- **Church Articles:** Named new church members or invitations to special services or events.

- **Job Ads:** If you don't know your ancestors occupation, the "Positions Wanted" section can be very useful. In this example, I wanted to know my grandmother's occupation. She had just moved from Brooklyn to Oakland, California in 1910 and I suspected that she was looking for work. Lo and behold, an ad that she had placed popped up that stated that she had stenography and typing skills and was looking for work in the legal profession. Even her address and phone number was included in the ad!

- **Legal Notices:** Did your ancestors have a business? Transfer a business? File bankruptcy? I have had all of those situations with my ancestors. In one example, my grandfather's business was sold to his two sons and the article was found in the legal section.

- **Letters to the Editor:** Was your ancestor outspoken? Did they often write a letter to the editor that was published?

- **Lodges, Clubs, and Societies:** Was your ancestor a member or an officer in a lodge or club? There were sections in old newspapers that had meeting schedules and articles about elections of officers. Often, in an obituary, the deceased's membership in a lodge was mentioned.

- **Missing Persons:** Since in the 19th century telephones were certainly not abundant, stories about missing persons were often written.

- **Politics:** In older newspapers, precinct captains and precinct workers were named; several of my own ancestors participated in helping people vote.

- **Real Estate Transactions:** Often titled this or "Recorder's Office", this may give you insight as to buying and selling of land and property by your ancestors.

- **Sports Results and Baseball Box Scores:** Did your ancestors play sports? There might be articles in the Sports section. If they played baseball at any level, there might be a situation where their names show up in a box score. My dad did and was mentioned frequently. And a citation of a female relative's hole in one in golf was in an article.

- **State or County Fair Winners:** Did your ancestor enter food, livestock, plants, or crafts at the fair? Lists of winners and their submittals and awards are listed.

- **Taxes Owed:** Often lists of taxes owed to the city or county are listed. It is surprising to find an ancestor owing three dollars to the county for taxes.

- **Vacations:** Before the advent of air conditioning, in warmer climes, folks would travel to resorts, springs, and other spots and the names of the travelers were often listed.

10 Clever Ways to Find More Ancestor Articles

- **Browse for Cause of Death** for up to two weeks prior to death date from obituary for an article about illness or accident

- **Combine Names** with occupations, business names, clubs, churches, etc. in your search criteria

- **Deliberately Misspell When Searching Online:** OCR is not perfect and scanning 100 year old newsprint creates errors

- **Married Women went by the Husband's Name:** So you are likely to find "Mildred Jones" as "Mrs. Samuel Jones"

- **Remember to Search Hyphenated Words:** In the old days, many words were hyphenated, so search portions of names or events

- **Search for an Address Rather than a Name** or combine address or just street name with surname

- **Searching for Birth Announcement?** Then add "born to" or "born to the wife of" to surname

- **Try Abbreviations** for given names, such as "Wm" for William, or "Jon" for John, or "Jos" for Joseph, and "Robt" for Robert

- **When Searching for Obituaries** add "beloved" or "dear" or "loving" in your online search criteria

- **Visit The Ancestor Hunt** at TheAncestorHunt.com/newspapers.html to get hundreds of articles and links to help you become a master newspaper researcher

21 Do's and Don'ts When Researching Newspapers

Remember to do the following.

- **DO** misspell search criteria words on purpose. The OCR process, converting images to text, create letters from dots, not just words

- **DO** search in the nearest big city or county seat

- **DO** add the word (s) beloved, dear, or loving to help find obituaries

- **DO** a search with syllables rather than whole words to take advantage of the significant use of hyphenated words in older newspapers

- **DO** take advantage of free trials with subscription newspaper sites before you buy

- **DO** use abbreviations, such as Wm, Jos, Eliz, Ave, or Sgt, etc. in your search criteria

- **DO** search for husbands name with Mrs. for married women

- **DO** a search for a few weeks prior to death date in the newspaper for hospitalization, illness or accident - helps determine the cause of death

- **DO** try to exchange a "b" for an "h", or a "c" for an "e' and many other combinations since they are very similar to the OCR process many times

- **DO** search for a street address. You might be surprised.

- **DO** have fun. It's rewarding to find out that your great uncle was shot at.

Avoid doing the following.

- **DON'T** just select a newspaper subscription database just because it's on sale

- **DON'T** assume that the newspaper collection has what you want just because the title is from your chosen city or town. Check the collection's date range

- **DON'T** assume that the cemetery stated in the obituary has not changed since the obituary has been published

- **DON'T** assume that the published obituary location is only published in the newspaper where death has occurred

- **DON'T** search just surnames

- **DON'T** just search U.S. newspapers based on ethnicity. Search newspapers in the ancestor's homeland

- **DON'T** rush out and purchase a subscription to newspaper collections. Libraries often subscribe to the same pay sites and if you have a library card, you may be able to search from home!

- **DON'T** assume that a wedding happened because your ancestor is listed in the Marriage Licenses Issued section. Cold feet does happen!

- **DON'T** assume that because an obituary states someone is a "native of" a place that they were born there.

- **DON'T** Ever. Give. Up.

33 Things You Can Find About Your Ancestors in Newspapers

- **Advertisements:** Local residents were quoted as having been cured by a variety of "interesting" remedies. Often photos and other descriptive information were included.

- **Anniversary Celebrations:** 25 and 50 year anniversaries often were rewarded with an article announcing the accomplishment, as well as a recounting of the celebration party and the attendees.

- **Birth Announcements:** Although the child is rarely named, his parents are and that can be helpful, especially if a child only lived a few years and you have the death announcement.

- **Church Articles:** Naming new church members or invitations to special services or events.

- **City and County Government Meetings:** Minutes of meetings are published and names are mentioned of the commissioners or supervisors as well as those who have conducted business during the meeting. If your ancestor had a claim due from the government entity for work performed, these lists are also available often.

- **Classified Ads:** Often you can find your ancestors names in the "want ads" as either selling something or, if they owned a business, trying to hire a new employee.

- **Death Notices and Obituaries:** Obvious help to researchers to name children, siblings, "native of" information, etc.

- **Divorce Proceedings:** Lists of couples who were in the various stages of divorce are often listed in the Vital Statistics section.

- **Engagement Announcements:** Often an announcement of an upcoming wedding would be found in the society page and many times a photo of the bride-to-be.

- **Land Applications and Sales:** Generally in the legal section, these might include notices from the Department of Interior.

- **Legal Notices:** Did your ancestors get divorced or sell or transfer a business? These are often found in legal notices, including bankruptcy or other legal matters, including wills and estates.

- **Letters to the Editor:** Was your ancestor outspoken? Did they often write a letter to the editor of the paper that was published?

- **Local Crime:** In addition to articles about the more serious or "colorful" crimes, there often are listings of more petty crimes, such as burglaries or home/business break-ins.

- **Lodges and Clubs:** Announcements of new members, or officer lists as well as upcoming meeting schedules are often published.

- **Mail:** List of unclaimed mail can often be found in smaller town newspapers. Useful to determine if your ancestor had moved away.

- **Marriage Licenses and Announcements:** When a license is issued, usually the names and addresses of the couple are mentioned. Also when the wedding occurs, often the event is listed as well, but not always. And of course there may be a detailed article about the wedding with a citing of many of the attendees.

- **Military Articles:** Did your ancestor join the Army or go to war? Often there are articles about them, as well as where they were stationed and promotions they may have received.

- **Missing Persons:** Since in the 19th century telephones were certainly not abundant, stories about missing persons were often written.

- **Out of Area Travelers:** Many older newspapers welcomed temporary residents with their names in the paper, listing the hotels they were staying in, their permanent residence (city), as well as the families they were visiting if they were staying in their home.

- **Personal Notices:** Illnesses, visitors, celebrations of all   kinds are often mentioned in the Society section.

- **Political Cartoons:** In the 19th century, photographs were rarely included in newspapers, so drawings of the likenesses of people were included, especially for politicians. I have several of these for one of my ancestors who was a State Senator.

- **Politics:** In older newspapers, precinct captains and precinct workers were named; several of my own ancestors participated in helping people vote.

- **Professional Directory:** Was your ancestor a doctor, lawyer, nurse, contractor, or embalmer? They might be found in these directories which are frequently published.

- **Real Estate Transactions and Transfers:** Did your ancestor transfer real estate to another family member or buy/sell a property?

- **School Graduations:** Lists of graduates are often listed for as early as elementary school through high school and college.

- **School News:** Lists of honor roll members, and other school events.

- **Society:** In smaller towns and even larger cities, the society pages listed attendees at parties of all kinds.

- **Sports:** If an ancestor was an athlete of any kind—possibly he would be cited in a baseball box score for college, high school or a local semi-pro team; or in an article regarding many other sports.

- **State or County Fair Winners:** Did your ancestor enter food, livestock, plants, or crafts at the fair? Lists of winners and their submittals and awards are listed.

- **Taxes Owed:** Often lists of taxes owed to the city or county are listed. It is surprising to find an ancestor owing 3 dollars to the county for taxes.

- **Theater and Television:** Lists of actors and actresses in vaudeville, other theater as well as early television are often mentioned in articles. These articles add depth to their life stories.

- **Union Activities:** Lists of trade union officers are often mentioned as well as their activities and scheduled meetings.

- **Vacations:** Before the advent of air conditioning, in warmer climes, folks would travel to resorts, springs, and other spots and the names of the travelers were often listed.

4 Challenges in Downloading Historical Newspaper Articles

I have been researching online historical newspaper sites for several years, both the free ones as well as the subscription-based sites. Their software capabilities, independent of the size and quality of their scanned collections, break down into two parts:

- How do you search the site and find "stuff"

- How do you download and save the articles that you find

This post is all about the second part – how do you download and save materials.

If you remember only ONE thing about this Research Tip it is this:

"Make sure you plan ahead before you download an article."

Many of these sites use different underlying base software and they all are quite different in their approach to providing a download capability.

Among the varying features that I have found will require you to do one or a combination of the items below:

- Download a .pdf of the page that contains your desired article.

- Download a .jpg of the page that contains your desired article.

- Use a software snipping tool such as the Windows "Snipping Tool" or some commercial offerings, such as SnagIt, Shutter, Jing, etc. There are many of these tools. So you just snip the article with this tool.

- The newspaper library software will snip the article for you and present it as a "whole" article.

- The newspaper library software will snip the article for you and present it in several pieces that comprise the entire article, such as the headline, and each paragraph as an independent .jpg file

The concern with all of these methods is

"How do you end up with a complete article that is large enough to read or is zoomable?"

"Zoomability" is one of the biggest complaints that I hear from my fellow online historical newspaper researchers after they download an article.

The four challenges regarding downloading an article and ending up with what you want and need are presented below.

- **Highlights:** Almost every online site presents the selected article after a search with highlighted search terms. So, depending on the capabilities provided by the site software, make sure that if you do NOT want to download the article with the highlighted text, that you download the article the way that you want it. There is always a way to get the article without the highlights. Experiment with the software or just download the whole page and crop your article later.

- **Chopped Up Articles:** A few of the sites will present the article in a "chopped up" format, depending on the length of the article. Usually, the title or headline is separated from the text, and if it is a long article, there may be several parts. So just like your need to concern yourself with downloading highlighted text, you will need to be careful with downloading articles that are broken up. It is safest to download the article (or entire page) in .pdf format and crop to your liking later. With .pdf formats you can generally zoom to the size you desire and then crop or snip the article in one piece.

- **The Article is Too Small:** This is the challenge that requires the most forethought when saving the article for later use. Much of the time, the repository software will allow you to download or snip articles in several different ways. Unfortunately, if you do not check your downloaded image before you leave the site, you might be disappointed in the size or the quality of said download. Make sure that it is either zoomable after the download or if not, that the article is zoomed to a readable size prior to downloading. Also, if it is too small when downloaded, depending on how the site prepares the clipping, zooming later may degrade the quality so that when zoomed, it is so fuzzy that you can't read it. Just like the other challenges, forethought will lead to the best results. It is always safest to download the article (or entire page) in .pdf format and crop to your liking later.

- **Oops, I Forgot the Citation:** This is easily the biggest mistake one can make and creates many "smack your head" moments. When I first started searching newspapers, I got so excited when I found an interesting article that I just downloaded the article and did not record the details about the newspaper where I found it. In order for me to find the article again for those that I discovered online I will need to perform all those searches again. Many of the repositories have a function or a link where the source details are presented. What I do is include the publication title, publication date and page number as part of the file name of the downloaded .pdf or image file.

The moral of the story is that online newspaper collections can be an incredibly valuable tool for your research. Fortunately, much of what is written above, and the challenges presented are not huge to overcome. Just think ahead and make sure that the articles that you download are readable, and in a format and size that pleases you and your future readers. And make sure you document where the articles came from!

The easiest way is to save the entire page as a pdf and include the citation info in the file name.

8 Ways to Not Screw Up Your Newspaper Search

Finding information and articles in newspapers about your ancestors is incredibly rewarding. And the amount of information about your ancestors in old newspapers is likely more than we can find.

But if you are not careful you can make assumptions about what is in ink on the newsprint and foul up your research because of poor conclusions. And it is easy to do, correct? We fall into the trap of assuming that if it is published then it must be right. So let's be careful out there.

Here are 8 ways to not screw up:

- **The "Native of" Trap:** Just because the obituary states that your ancestor was a "native of" Boston, Massachusetts doesn't mean that they were born there. She may have lived there for decades, or maybe her parents moved there when she was 3 months old and everyone assumed she was born there. So just because the obit states the city that she was a "native of" does not mean she was born there.

- **The Marriage Trap:** There is a section in the Vitals area of the newspapers for Marriage Licenses. So your ancestor or research target is listed there with their intended spouse. Guess what—the operative word is "intended." Just because they got a license does not mean that a wedding took place. You have more research to do.

- **The Divorce Trap:** Divorces Filed and Interlocutory Decrees are often listed in the Vital Statistics section of the newspaper. But those are NOT Divorces. Only Divorces Granted count as an actual divorce.

- **The Border Trap:** Don't assume that all articles are going to be in the newspapers of the state of residence for your ancestor. If your target lived near the state border, check out neighboring state newspapers. For example, if they lived in Council Bluffs, Iowa, check out the Omaha, Nebraska papers. Or if they lived in Camden, New Jersey, check out the Philadelphia newspapers.

- **The Human-Interest Story Bonus (and Possible Trap):** Interesting articles were copied all over the country. My 3rd great uncle obtained possession of Geronimo's knife and the article was in papers in several states as a human-interest story. Make sure that stories such as these state the actual location of the subject. Don't assume that it is the location of the newspaper that you are reading.

- **The Marriage Trap (Part 2):** If you are searching for a woman, don't just search for her given name and married surname. Often women who were adults and married were written as Mrs. Robert Smith rather than Gladys Smith for example. So, unless she was a widow, unmarried, was divorced, or a child, you likely won't find her by searching for her given name.

- **The Burial Trap:** Just because the obituary states that burial is to take place at Mountain View Cemetery doesn't mean that they were actually buried there. There may have been a last-minute change of plans by the family. Or Mountain View was later closed and the gravestones and remains were moved to another cemetery.

- **The Always Spell Correctly Trap:** When typing in your search criteria into that little box in the online newspaper database remember something very important. You are searching against an index that was created from hardware and software processes that scanned the newspaper and attempted to convert the ink dots on the paper to a letter and thus words. There is no spell check that converts those ink dots into words or actual names.

The bottom line is that one should not assume that everything in the newspaper is correct. These examples are just a few where improper conclusions can lead to documenting inaccurate facts and furthermore, wasting time in future research.

Use Abbreviations to Find 50% More Newspaper Articles

Introduction

- **What?** Use an abbreviation instead of a full word

- **Why?** Typesetters used abbreviations to save space

- **How?** Enter the abbreviation in your search criteria

- **Result?** Find hidden articles - Usually 50% more pertinent hits

Consider these common abbreviations in your searches.

- Ave for Avenue

- Benj for Benjamin

- Capt for Captain

- Chas for Charles

- Co for Company

- Col for Colonel

- Corp for Corporation

- Cpl for Corporal

- Eliz for Elizabeth

- Genl for General

- Geo for George

- Inc for Incorporated

- Jas for James

- Jno for John

- Jos for Joseph

- Ln for Lane

- Margt for Margaret

- NYC for New York City

- Pl for Place

- Pres for President

- Robt for Robert

- Saml for Samuel

- Sgt for Sergeant

- St for Street

- Thos for Thomas

- Wm for William

Include these abbreviations in your search criteria and you will find hidden articles and get as much as 50% more pertinent hits.

Analyze the Newspaper Vitals Section

The Vitals section of the newspaper is the most pursued by genealogy newspaper researchers – primarily because that is where death notices and obituaries reside.

But there are more than just obits in this important section. Below is a list of the keys to getting the most for your family history research out of the Vitals section.

- **Generally, deaths, marriages and marriage licenses, births and divorce actions** are in the same section of the newspaper. Sometimes they are categorized as "Vitals" or "Vital Statistics" but many times are headlined by the individual categories. In many newspapers they tend to be on the same numbered page from day to day, which can help you if you are browsing.

- **The key to analyzing an obituary is to examine EVERY single word.** It is easy to skip over parts of the notice if one is not careful, and there are gems of info if you are thorough. I have missed important pieces of info because of the sheer excitement in finding the obit in the first place. The three steps should be find, cite, and analyze.

- **Remember that just because a couple is listed in the "Marriage Licenses" section does NOT mean that they got married.** Go ahead if you want to and record the date of the license but do not record it as a marriage unless you have proof of said marriage.

- **Divorces filed and interlocutory decrees** are often listed in the Vitals section. But they are NOT final divorces. Only Divorces Granted count as an actual divorce.

- **The way that the divorce is phrased** can tell you who filed for divorce. For example Anna from Carl means that Anna filed; Carl from Anna the reverse.

- **Dates for births are not always stated correctly.** For example, most of the time a birth announcement will tell you the date of birth, but then others will just list the event, the gender, and the name of the father. Do not assume that if the date is not stated that it is the date of the publication of the newspaper.

- **Obituaries often do not have the date of death**. Similar to the birth example, do not assume that the death date is the date of publication. Often it will say "last Monday." Make sure that you use the proper calendar to ascertain the exact date.

- **Marriage licenses do not usually give the date of issuance**. Generally, "Married" or "Marriages" do. If the date is missing do not assume that it is the date of newspaper publication.

- **I have seen Marriage Licenses also titled "Intention to Wed."** Make sure that you record the address and/or city of each of the couple. Sometimes if one is from a different locale, that will give you a hint as to previous residency and maybe birth location.

- **Regarding locations** make sure that you do not assume in an obituary that "native of" means the birth location of the deceased. That is not always the case.

- **After you have found an obituary and cite the source**, you can start the analysis process. But remember that often obituaries were republished sometimes for a few days after the first publication. More importantly, some obituaries were changed in later publications, when some family members were omitted in the first version. This can often happen if the deceased had multiple marriages and children of these marriages.

- **Funeral notices and "In Remembrance"** were also included in the Vitals section. Check to make sure that the funeral location was not changed from the original location stated in the obituary. And In Remembrance articles were often published on the anniversary of death – helpful if you don't have the death date or the original obituary.

Newspaper Subscription Considerations

Finding information and articles in newspapers about your ancestors is incredibly rewarding. And the amount of information about your ancestors in old newspapers is likely more than we can find. If you follow TheAncestorHunt.com, you know that I am "big" on using old newspapers as resources to find about your family and their stories. There are over 40,000 links to free titles at TheAncestorHunt.com/newspapers.html.

But what about the paid newspaper subscription sites? I have used the three large ones in the U.S. (Newspapers.com, NewspaperArchive, and GenealogyBank). There are other sites where newspapers are available, such as Ancestry.com, British Newspaper Archive, FindMyPast, MyHeritage, etc. There are pluses and minuses to all of these sites, but this article is not a comparison of these sites.

- **Why is that you ask?** In my opinion, each person should make up their own mind as to what characteristics are important to them and how each of these sites fit your particular preferences.

- **What are the five most important characteristics?** Here's what I believe are those that you should consider:

- **User Interface and Searching Features:** Every site mentioned above (and those not mentioned) have different user interfaces. Some are simple and easy to figure out and use; some have richer capabilities and features. I always like to try the "Advanced Search" features because that generally indicates the total breadth of capability. And one MUST read the Help documentation for each of these sites. Generally they will let you know what type of search criteria can be entered; for example Boolean and proximity searches. Quite honestly I have heard many subscribers complain about not finding anything when they haven't even tried to learn all the search capabilities available to them.

- **Scan and OCR Quality:** The index that the site has created is only as good as the quality of the original scan and the OCR software that they use to build the index. Were the newspapers scanned from originals or from microfilm, or from copies of microfilm? Some of the collections that I have seen have an extremely poor quality image displayed after selecting a search result. This indicates to me that the original image that they applied the OCR process to was degraded and hence the index certainly will suffer. In other words, your ancestor is mentioned but the scan was so lousy that the OCR process could not build an acceptable index entry with the correct spelling of the name.

- **Price and Billing Practices:** Some of the aforementioned sites are 4 times as expensive as the others. Some have a monthly plan, some annually only. Some auto-renew and some do not. If you purchase a subscription it is incumbent on you to read the terms of the subscription as well as the fine print. As always with any purchase online, it is buyer-be AWARE. Many have a free trial period, which gives you a chance to try before you buy a long term subscription.

- **Collections Available:** Just as in Real Estate where the motto is "Location, location, location" the motto for subscription newspaper research sites is "Database, database, database." I get asked all the time if someone should purchase a subscription to site A. I always ask them first for the states, cities, or areas that they are researching, as well as the dates that their ancestors lived there, does the site have a collection of newspapers available? If it doesn't for a preponderance of your ancestors—if you purchase a subscription don't complain when you can't find anything. All sites have a list of what newspapers and dates are in their collections. Check those out before you buy.

- **Image Downloads:** This is critical. Can you download just the image? Can you download the entire page in pdf? How zoomable is the image or pdf after you download it? The reason this is critical is because some of the sites do not have an image or pdf that allows you to zoom to make a larger image without distortion. I find this unsatisfactory when snipping obituary notices which tend to be quite small in size: and if there is distortion after making the obit larger, one can't read it.

Most sites have some sort of free trial or a short time subscription so you don't have to plunk down money for a whole year if your resources are tight and you just want to check out the site.

So, check out free old newspaper resources but don't forget these historical newspaper subscription sites – they have different collections available than those on the free sites. Your family history research will be enhanced by using all the resources available to you.

Use Nicknames to Find More Ancestor Newspaper Articles

Introduction

- **What?** Use a nickname instead of full given name

- **Result?** Get as much as 50% more pertinent hits

Consider these frequently used nicknames in your searches.

- Abigail, Tabitha..Abbie, Abby

- Abraham..Abe, Abra

- Alexander ....Alec, Alex

- Alexander ....Sandy

- Alice..Allie

- Alice..Elsie

- Antoinette, Henrietta...Nettie

- Archibald ....Arch, Archie

- August..Gus

- Augustus...Augie

- Bartholomew...Bart, Bat

- Catherine, Katherine..Kitty

- Caroline..Callie, Carrie

- Charlotte...Lollie, Lottie

- Christopher..Kit

- Clarissa, Clarinda ....Clara

- Cornelius...Con

- Cyrus ....Si, Cy

- Dorothy...Dolly, Dot

- Edith .... Edie

- Edwin, Edward .... Ned

- Eleanor, Ellen, Helen .... Nellie

- Elizabeth .... Bess, Betsey

- Florence .... Flora, Flossie

- Frances .... Fanny, Frankie

- Hamilton .... Ham

- Harold, Henry .... Hal

- Harriet .... Hatty, Hattie

- Helen .... Nellie

- Henrietta .... Etta, Nettie

- Henry .... Hank

- Henry .... Harry

- Hiram .... Hy

- Isaac .... Ike

- Jackson, John .... Jack

- Jacob .... Jake

- Janet, Virginia .... Jenny

- Jedidiah .... Jed

- Josiah, Cyrus .... Si, Cy

- Katherine, Kathleen .... Kate, Kay

- Louetta .... Etta

- Malachi, Malcolm .... Mal

- Margaret .... Meg, Maggie, Peggy

- Margaret, Margery .... Madge

- Martha .... Mattie, Patsy

- Martha, Mary, Amelia .... Mollie
- Martha, Patience...Patty
- Mary ....Mamie, Polly
- Mary, Wilhelmina ....Minnie
- Mindwell, Wilhelmina ....Mina
- Nathaniel... Nat, Nate
- Newton...Newt
- Oliver..Olli
- Patrick .... Paddy
- Phineas...Finney
- Richard .... Dick
- Sarah .... Sadie, Sally
- Tabitha...Abbie, Abby
- Thaddeus...Tad
- Virgil .... Virg
- Virginia ....Jenny
- Wiley, William ....Willie
- Winifred, Edwina..Winnie

Search Hyphenated Words for 30% More Results

Finding your ancestors in newspaper articles is in my opinion – an art, not a science. You must be clever and resourceful to get around the quality limitations in old newspapers. A "feature" of older newspapers is the use of the hyphen. Hyphenated words were often used heavily to save space and due to the limitations of fixed-width type.

The bottom line is that if you search for a portion of your ancestor's surname (or any other word, not necessarily a name), rather than the entire word, you may get additional results. For example, if your ancestor's name was "Jorgenson" try searching for "Jorgen." The typesetter may have split the word so that at the end of one line are the letters "Jorgen-" with the hyphen, and the next line may start with "son". I have an ancestral line with the surname "Braunhart." Many times, an article may have a line that ends with "Braun-" and the next line starts with "hart." This creates some additional challenges, just like "Williamson" may be split up as "William" and "son." The first and second set of letters end up being a very common set of syllables so your results may be too numerous to be of much help.

> Rufus Hatch—"Uncle Rufe" as he is known in New York—addressed a letter to *The Hour* last Saturday giving the true inwardness of the passenger war—all the roads have lost heavily and show greatly reduced receipts. The Vanderbilt roads make no reports, but it is suspected that they feel the war quite as much as the others. There are two exceptions—the Reading and the Louisville and Nashville.
>
> The *Washington Republican* says: "There is no other city on the continent where it is so easy for a young man of good address to get appointed to the position of a son-in-law to a gentleman of wealth and standing as it is in Washington during the season. And this sort of appointment is really more desirable than that of Consul in a warm climate." If there is a stampede of bachelors to the National Capital, the *Republican's* paragraph will be to blame.

Here is an example of how often hyphens have been used. In this case, six times in two short paragraphs!

That's over 30% of the lines! So, if you don't search for the hyphenated words, you could lose up to 30% of the potential results.

Here are three examples that show the different uses of the hyphen. And always consider that the "break" may not always be in the logical place in the word.

> An unidentified man stepped in front of a moving car at the corner of East First and Los Angeles streets yesterday afternoon, and was knocked to the ground, sustaining a deep three-inch laceration of the scalp, with possibly a fracture of the skull.
>
> The man was under the influence of liquor at the time, say witnesses to the accident, who reported that he left a saloon a moment before he was struck by the car and attempted to cross the tracks, unmindful of the approaching car. Inmates of the saloon say that his name is believed to be William Patterson, but no one who knew him could be found.

In this sample, you could search for "Patter" when your target name was "Patterson."

> At Hotel Hollywood Mr. and Mrs.
> Arthur Letts gave a large dinner party
> last evening. Christmas bells and red
> satin ribbon were arranged in canopy
> effect over the table and holly and
> ferns decorated the table. Covers were
> laid for Mr. and Mrs. Harry Philp, Mr.
> and Mrs. C. B. Weaver, Mr. and Mrs.
> J. W. Aldritt, Rev. and Mrs. A. Har-
> die, Mrs. Richard Letts, Misses Ethel
> Hardie, Ada, Edna and Gladys Letts,
> Lila and Dorothy Weaver, Dr. W. S.
> Philp, Masters Harland Weaver, Cyril
> Aldrit and Arthur Letts, jr.

In this sample, even a short word like "Hardie" is split up, so you would search for "Har." This may lead to too many results but is worth a try.

> WASHINGTON, Dec. 25.—Because
> of the prisoner's previous good mili-
> tary record the president has issued a
> pardon in the case of Paul H. McDon-
> ald, formerly first lieutenant of the
> Tenth Infantry. He was convicted
> about a year ago on the charge of ob-
> taining money under false pretenses
> and sentenced to be dismissed from the
> army and to serve two years in the
> military prison at Fort Leavenworth,
> Kas.

In this last sample, I wouldn't think that the name would be split this way but searching for "McDon" and "ald" may lead to many more results. Be open-minded about where the split may occur.

Don't give up and remember that hyphenated words give you opportunities for additional searches, and if the search criteria is carefully crafted, many more results.

The Best Way to Find HIDDEN Ancestor Newspaper Articles

Introduction

- **What?** Deliberately misspell your search criteria

- **Why?** Optical Character Recognition (OCR)—converting images to text, is not perfect and 100-year-old newsprint is full of errors

- **How?** Change the letters in your search criteria

- **Result?** Find hidden articles; up to 20% more pertinent hits

The following letter and character pairs are often confused.

- , (comma) and l (lowercase L), I (capital i), or 1 (the number one)

- 0 (zero) and O (capital letter O)

- c and e

- Capital B and 8

- Capital D and G

- Capital D and O

- Capital G and 6

- Capital H and B

- Capital K and |<

- Capital R and B

- Capital S and 5

- Capital S and 8

- Capital Z and 2

- d and cl

- e and o

- h and b

- h and k

- h and n

- i, l, 1, /, !, and I (lowercase i, lowercase L, number one, slash, & capital I)

- n and ri (en and ar eye)

- nl and m (en el and em)

- r and n

- rn and m (ar n and em)

- v and y

Deliberately misspell your search criteria using these patterns and you will find hidden articles, getting up to 20% more pertinent hits.

The Easiest Way to Find Historical Newspapers in America

The fact is that all old newspapers ever published in the United States are not online. Much less than you might think.

What is your guess of the percentage? 10%? 20%? 5%? No, the answer (at least with respect to Chronicling America) is that there are approximately 3,500 online titles and there have been over 156,000 titles ever published in the U.S. That yields just a tad over 2.2%. That's not much, is it?

Of course, Chronicling America doesn't represent all of the online titles and digitized pages available. My research results in about 37,000 free online links for the U.S. So, 37,000 (online) in comparison to 156,000 (published) – that's about 24% of the titles. What about some of the paid sites, such as GenealogyBank, Newspaper.com, etc.? GenealogyBank on their website claims over 13,000 titles and Newspapers dot com states 20,000. And that doesn't count Newspaper Archive, MyHeritage, or FindMyPast's collections. And there is considerable overlap probably.

So, if we are being generous, let's add another 15% for the paid sites. That says that 30% have been digitized. That's titles, NOT pages. A single title that has one page from one issue in our math example counts the same as a title published daily for every year for a hundred years. The moral of the story is that with all the date gaps that we newspaper researchers run into – it is almost impossible to figure out how much indeed has been digitized.

So, let's just say for now that 15 to 30% of all U.S. newspaper pages have been digitized. Personally, I think that's a very high number, but......

That leaves about 70-85% that are NOT online! Now, what the heck do we do? Offline research – that's what. And the Library of Congress helps us out with the US Newspaper Directory from 1690 to Present so we can do offline research (ChroniclingAmerica.loc.gov/search/titles). This handy directory provides not just multiple ways to find newspapers published, but tons of facts about those newspapers. Just do your choice of searches from the main US Newspaper Directory from 1690 to Present page. Here's an example of a "fact" page".

About The villager. (New York [N.Y.]) 1933-current
New York [N.Y.] (1933-current)

About | Libraries that Have It | MARC Record

Title:
The villager. : (New York [N.Y.]) 1933-current

Place of publication:
New York [N.Y.]

Geographic coverage:
- Brooklyn, Kings, New York | View more titles from this: City County, State
- Greenwich Village, New York, New York | View more titles from this: City County, State
- New York, New York, New York | View more titles from this: City County, State

Publisher:
W.G. Bryan and Associates

Dates of publication:
1933-current

Description:
- Vol. 1, no. 1 (Apr. 13, 1933)-

Frequency:
Weekly

Language:
- English

Subjects:
- Brooklyn (New York, N.Y.)--Newspapers.
- Greenwich Village (New York, N.Y.)--Newspapers.
- Kings County (N.Y.)--Newspapers.
- New York (N.Y.)--Newspapers.
- New York (State)--Kings County.--fast--(OCoLC)fst01220099
- New York (State)--New York County.--fast--(OCoLC)fst01234953
- New York (State)--New York--Brooklyn.--fast--(OCoLC)fst01312516
- New York (State)--New York--Greenwich Village.--fast--(OCoLC)fst01322891
- New York (State)--New York.--fast--(OCoLC)fst01204333
- New York County (N.Y.)--Newspapers.

Notes:
- "A weekly newspaper reflecting the finest traditions of Washington Square and Greenwich Village."
- Available on microfilm from New York Public Library (1933-1985).
- Latest issue consulted: Vol. 70, no. 22 (Sept. 20, 2000).
- Published at: New York, N.Y., <1933>; Greenwich Village, N.Y. <1947>; Brooklyn, N.Y., <Dec. 14, 1989->; New York, N.Y., <1999->.
- Publishers: W.G. Bryan and Associates, <1933>; Bryan Publications, <1947>; Serif Press, <Dec. 14, 1989->; Community Media LLC, <Sept. 1999->

LCCN:
sn 83030608

OCLC:
9548003

ISSN:
0042-6202

Related Links:
- http://www.thevillager.com/

Holdings:
☉ View complete holdings information

See all the interesting information about the paper? If you had an ancestor from the area that you think might be mentioned in this paper, and the paper was not online, maybe you could find it at an archive or library in original form or microfilm. From this "facts" page, you can actually find out where the newspaper is held. Just click on the "View complete holdings information" link at the bottom.

Here are some of the results for this newspaper:

Libraries that Have It: The villager. (New York [N.Y.]) 1933-current
New York [N.Y.] (1933-current)

About | Libraries that Have It | MARC Record

HOLDING: Cornell Univ, Ithaca, NY
○ View more titles from this institution

Available as: Unspecified
Last updated: 03/2014

HOLDING: Franklin D Roosevelt Libr, Hyde Park, NY
○ View more titles from this institution

Available as: Microfilm Service Copy
Dates:

- s=<1945:4:19>

Last updated: 05/1991

HOLDING: New York Hist Soc, Newsp Proj, New York, NY
○ View more titles from this institution

Available as: Original
Scattered issues wanting

Dates:

- <1933:4:13, 5:25-1934:5:3,17-6:14,28-8:16,30-9:27>
- <1934:10:11-25, 11:8-12:6,20-1935:7:11>
- <1935:8:1-11:21, 12:5-1936:2:20, 3:5-7:16, 8:6, 9:24-10:22>
- <1936:12:17-1937:4:15>
- <1937:5:6-1961:6:8,28-7:20, 8:3-24, 9:28-10:12-26, 11:9>
- <1961:11:23-1963:1:24, 2:7-5:16,30-7:25, 8:8-1964:9:17>

Last updated: 09/1992

So, you can see that it is available for your browsing pleasure at several libraries and archives—both in original and in microfilm form. Don't give up if your paper of interest is not online. Visit the US Newspaper Directory from 1690 to Present from the Library of Congress. Good Luck; persistence will win out.

Chronicling America: Mastering the Advanced Search

There are two methods to search the Library of Congress "Chronicling America" (ChroniclingAmerica.LOC.gov) for historical newspapers.

1) Basic Search, available from the Home Page as well as the "Search Pages" tab, allows you to enter your search criteria, and restrict results to a single state and to a range of years.

2) The Advanced Search, which I highly recommend that you use most if not all of the time, has TEN different fields that you can enter that will allow you to narrow your search. Below the image is a description of each of these fields and how to use them.

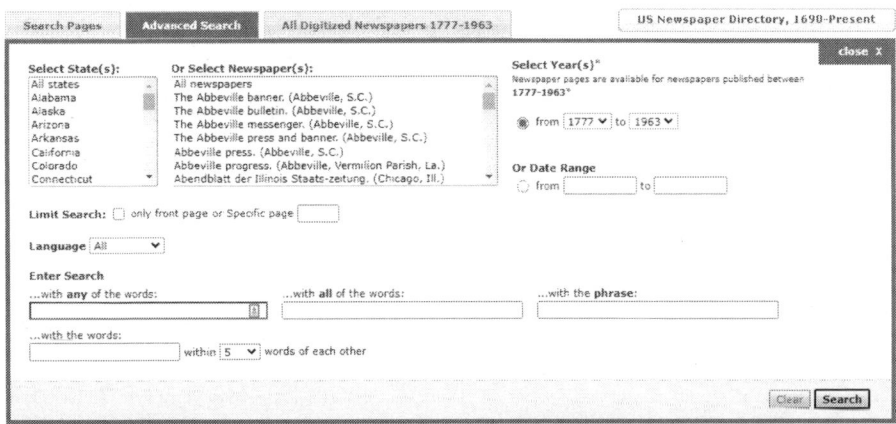

- **Select State:** One or more states can be selected, by holding the CTRL key and clicking on all of the states that you wish to search at one time; or you can choose "All states".

- **Select Newspaper(s):** You can select one or more (or all) newspapers from which to conduct the search. Note that selecting a state does not restrict the newspapers in this field, unfortunately.

- **Select Year(s):** You can restrict your results to a range of years; currently between 1777 and 1963 by choosing a "from" year followed by a "to" year.

- **Date Range:** You can restrict your results to a range of dates by choosing a "from" date followed by a "to" date.

- **Limit Search:** You can restrict your search to a specific page within the newspaper issue; for example, Front Pages, page 8s, etc. This is handy if you are looking for a specific section of a newspaper and it generally is on page 16, such as the Vitals Section for example.

- **Language:** You can restrict the newspapers searched by a specific language. Currently there are 19 languages available in the collection.

- **Enter Search with any of the words:** Similar to a Boolean "or", enter all of the words that you wish to search for. In this case, any occurrence of one or more of the words on a page will trigger a positive result.

- **Enter Search with all of the words:** Similar to a Boolean "and", enter all of the words that you wish to search for. In this case, all of the words must occur on a page in order for a positive result to be returned.

- **Enter Search with the phrase:** Similar to entering a phrase of more than one word encased in quotation marks. In this case, all of the words in the exact phrase must occur on a page in order for a positive result to be returned.

- **Enter Search with the words within X words of each other:** This is called a proximity search. In this case, you enter the words, and then select 5, 10, 50, or 100. This is handy if you are searching for more than one person, event, or subject, and also very useful when middle initials are used in people's names. For example, if you are searching for Franklin Roosevelt, a proximity search of 5 words would return pages with Franklin Delano Roosevelt or Franklin D. Roosevelt. A subject example is entering tax reform within 5 words. This would include results for any occurrence of tax reform, but also reform of income tax.

Notes

9. Occupations

What your ancestor did—was it for money or was it the
purpose of their life?

24 Places You Can Find Your Ancestors' Occupations

If you are like me, you want to know as much as possible about the lives of your ancestors. Determining their stories is a challenge, especially if there is no one alive who remembers the ancestor that you are researching.

But fortunately, there are several documents that record at least, the occupation of the target ancestor, and that can tell you a lot about the person.

Knowing how the ancestor worked tells you a lot about how they lived and possibly their standing in the community.

- **Alumni Directories**
- **Apprenticeship Records**
- **Birth Certificate/Record of child:** Parent occupations are often provided
- **Census Records**
- **City Directories**
- **Death Certificates**
- **Draft Cards**
- **Marriage Certificates**
- **Membership in Fraternal Societies**
- **Military Enlistment and Other Records**
- **Miscellaneous Court Documents**
- **Mortuary Records**
- **Naturalization Records**
- **Newspaper Articles of all kinds:** Legal notices, advertisements and classified ads are often useful

- **Obituaries**

- **Passenger Lists**

- **Passport Applications**

- **Patent Applications**

- **Photographs:** Although not written, may include a uniform that can be a good hint as to occupation

- **Recorded local and town histories**

- **Social Security Applications:** Employer's name is often included

- **Union Membership Documents**

- **Voter Registrations**

- **Wills/Probate**

280 Old Occupations Used in the Census and Newspapers

The following terms were used in the United States and United Kingdom.

- **Abactor:** Cattle Thief
- **Abigail:** Ladies Maid
- **Accipitary:** Falconer
- **Accomptant:** Accountant
- **Ackerman:** A Plowman or Oxherder
- **Ale Draper:** Seller of Beer and Ale
- **Alewife:** A Proprietor of a Tavern
- **All Spice:** Grocer
- **Almoner:** Giver of Charity to The Needy
- **Alnager:** A Wool Inspector
- **Amanuensis:** Secretary or Stenographer
- **Aproneer:** Shopkeeper
- **Artificer:** A Soldier Mechanic Who Does Repairs
- **Backmaker:** Cooper Who Makes Tubs, Barrels, and Buckets from Wood
- **Badger:** Licensed Pauper Who Wears A Badge as His Certificate
- **Bagman:** Traveling Salesman
- **Bailie:** Bailiff
- **Balister:** Archer
- **Bandster:** Worker Who Binds Wheat Bundles After Harvesting
- **Basil Worker:** Tanner Who Works with Goat and Sheep Hides
- **Batman:** A Military Officer's Personal Assistant
- **Baxter:** Baker
- **Biddy:** Female Servant
- **Bluestocking:** Female Writer

- **Boniface:** Keeper of An Inn
- **Bowyer:** A Bowmaker
- **Brazier:** One Who Works with Brass
- **Brewster:** Beer Manufacturer
- **Brightsmith:** Metal Worker
- **Burgomaster:** Mayor
- **Caddy Butcher:** Butcher Who Works Only in Horse Meant
- **Caffler:** Rag and Bone Man, Peddler
- **Calciner:** Worker Who Makes Lime from Powdered Bones
- **Calenderer:** Worker on The Calender Machine Used for Finishing Papers and Fabrics
- **Carder:** Spinning Mill Worker
- **Cardroomer:** Worker in The Carding Room of A Mill
- **Carnifex:** A Regular Butcher
- **Catchpole:** An official Who Pursues Those with Delinquent Debts
- **Caulker:** One Who Filled Up Cracks (In Ships or Windows or Seams)
- **Chaisemaker:** Carriage Maker
- **Chandler:** Candlemaker
- **Chevener:** Embroiderer of Fine Stockings
- **Chiffonnier:** Wig Maker
- **Claker:** Magician or Astrologer
- **Clark:** Clerk
- **Clerk:** Clergyman, Cleric
- **Cobbler:** A Shoemaker
- **Cohen:** Priest
- **Collier:** Coal Miner
- **Colporteur:** Peddler of Books
- **Cooper:** A Maker or Repairer of Barrels, Casks, and Tubs

- **Cordwainer:** Shoemaker

- **Costermonger:** Peddler of Fruits and Vegetables

- **Crocker:** Potter

- **Crowner:** Coroner

- **Currier:** A Leather Tanner, or A Horse Groom

- **Danter:** Female Overseer in Silk-Winding Room

- **Deal Porter:** Specialist Who Hauled Wood Between Ship and Shore

- **Delfman:** Salesman of Delft Pottery from Holland

- **Deviller:** Operator of The Machine Which Shreds Cloth at The Fabric Mill

- **Docker:** Dock Worker Who Load and Unloads Cargo

- **Doffer:** Worker Who Replaces Empty Loom Spools with Full Ones in The Weaving Industry

- **Dowser:** One Who Finds Water Using A Rod or Witching Stick

- **Dragoon:** Cavalryman

- **Draper:** A Dealer in Dry Goods

- **Drayman:** A Driver of A Heavy Freight Cart

- **Dresser:** A Surgeon's Assistant in A Hospital

- **Dripping Man:** Seller of Drippings (Fat)

- **Drover:** One Who Drives Cattle, Sheep, Etc. to Market

- **Drudge:** Menial Laborer

- **Drummer:** Traveling Salesman

- **Dubber:** Worker in Fabric Mill Who Raises The Nap of The Cloth

- **Duffer:** Peddler

- **Ealdorman:** Kings Court Deputy

- **Eggler:** An Egg Seller

- **Ellerman:** Seller of Lamp Oil

- **Enumerator:** Census Taker

- **Eremite:** Hermit
- **Estafette:** Mounted Courier
- **Eyer:** Worker Who Makes The Eyeholes in Needles
- **Factor:** Agent, Commission Merchant
- **Fanner:** Worker Who Winnows Grain
- **Farrier:** A Blacksmith, One Who Shoes Horses
- **Faulkner:** Falconer
- **Feather Mason:** Worker Who Splits Stone Using Steel Tools
- **Fell Monger:** Remover of Hair or Wool from Hides in Leather Making
- **Feller:** Woodcutter
- **Festitian:** Physician
- **Fiddler:** Clay Worker
- **Fish Bobber:** Mariner Who Ferries Fish Cargo from The Trawler to The Wharf
- **Fishmonger:** A Fish Seller
- **Flauner:** Confectioner
- **Fletcher:** Arrow Maker
- **Fossetmaker:** Worker Who Makes Taps for Kegs and Barrels
- **Fower:** Street Cleaner
- **Friezer:** One Who Embroiders Cloth with Silver and Gold
- **Fuller:** One Who Fulls Cloth
- **Galloon Maker:** Maker of Metal Trim for Military Uniforms
- **Gaoler:** Jailer
- **Gater:** Watchman
- **Gaunter:** Glovemaker
- **Glazier:** Window Glassman
- **Gorseman:** Seller of Gorse and Hay for Broom Making
- **Gossoon:** Servant Boy

- **Granger:** Farmer
- **Groover:** Miner
- **Haberdasher:** Seller of Clothing and/or Accessories
- **Hacker:** Maker of Hoes
- **Hairweaver:** Maker of Horsehair Cloth
- **Hatcheler:** One Who Combed Out or Carded Flax
- **Hawker:** A Peddler
- **Haymonger:** Dealer in Hay
- **Hayward:** An official Responsible for Fences and Hedges
- **Henchman:** Horseman or Groom
- **Higgler:** Itinerant Peddler
- **Hillier:** Roof Tiler
- **Hind:** Farm Laborer
- **Hobbler:** A Person Who Tows Boats on A Canal or River
- **Holster:** A Groom Who Took Care of Horses, often at An Inn
- **Hooker:** Reaper
- **Hooper:** One Who Made Hoops for Casks and Barrels
- **Horner:** Maker of Cutlery Handles Made of Horn
- **Hostler or Ostler:** Horse Groomer
- **Howdy Wife:** Midwife
- **Huckster:** Street Peddler
- **Hurrier:** Coal Haulers Who Work Underground Ferrying Coal
- **Husbandman:** Farmer
- **Ice Cutter:** Someone Who Saws Blocks of Ice for Refrigeration
- **Idleman:** Person Living Without Work and of Their Own Means
- **In-bye Worker:** Miner Who Works The Coalface
- **Ironmonger:** A Seller of Items Made of Iron
- **Jagger:** Fish Peddler

- **Jigger:** Potter Who Works to Shape The Bottoms of Pieces

- **Jinny (or Ginny):** Miner Who Operates The Ginny Carriage

- **Joiner:** Skilled Carpenter

- **Journeyman:** One Who Had Served His Apprenticeship and Mastered His Craft

- **Joyner/Joiner:** A Skilled Carpenter

- **Jute Preparer:** One Who Beat and Prepared Jute Plants Prior to Them Being Turned Into Rope

- **Kedger:** Fisherman

- **Keeler:** Bargeman

- **Kellogg:** Animal Slaughterer

- **Kempster:** Wool Comber

- **Knacker:** One Who Buys Animals or Animal Carcasses to Use as Animal Food or as Fertilizer

- **Kneller:** Chimney Sweep

- **Knocker-up:** A Professional Waker, Who Literally Knocks on Doors or Windows to Rouse People from Sleep

- **Knoller:** Bellringer

- **Lagger:** Sailor

- **Lamplighter:** Someone Who Lights, Extinguishes, and Refuels Gas Street Lamps

- **Lapidary:** A Jeweler

- **Lardner:** Keeper of The Cupboard

- **Laster:** Shoemaker

- **Lavender:** Washer Woman

- **Leach:** Doctor or Veterinarian

- **Leavelooker:** Food Inspector

- **Lector:** Someone Who Reads to Factory Workers for Entertainment

- **Lederer:** Leather Maker

- **Leech:** Physician
- **Leightonward:** Gardener
- **Limeburner:** Worker Who Processes Lime from Limestone By Burning
- **Linkerboy:** Man Who Carries A Lantern for Hire at Night
- **Log Driver:** Someone Who Floats and Guides Logs Downriver for Transportation
- **Longshoreman:** Stevedore
- **Lormer:** Maker of Horse Gear
- **Malender:** Farmer
- **Maltster:** Brewer
- **Manciple:** Steward
- **Mangler:** Worker Who Operates The Laundry Mangle
- **Marbler:** Worker Who Makes Paper Looked Marbled
- **Mason:** Bricklayer
- **Melder:** Corn Miller
- **Milliner:** Maker of Ladies' Hats
- **Mintmaster:** One Who Issued Local Currency
- **Misegatherer:** Local Tax Collector
- **Monger:** Seller of Goods (Ale, Fish)
- **Morroco:** Worker of Leather from Morroco
- **Mudlark:** Scavenger Specializing in Sweeping The Banks of Rivers at Low Tide
- **Muleskinner:** Teamster
- **Neatherder:** Herds Cows
- **ordinary Keeper:** Innkeeper
- **Ostler:** Groomsman at An Inn or An Innkeeper in General
- **Owler:** Wool Smuggler
- **Packman:** Peddler

- **Pantler:** Butler

- **Pardoner:** Salesman of official Church Pardons (Papal or Bishop)

- **Parminster:** Stone Roofer

- **Pattern Maker:** A Maker of A Clog Shod with An Iron Ring

- **Pedascule:** Schoolteacher

- **Peregrinator:** Itinerant Wanderer

- **Peruker:** Wigmaker

- **Pettifogger:** Shyster Lawyer

- **Pigman:** Crockery Dealer

- **Pinsetter:** Someone who sets bowling pins back up after each bowl

- **Plain Worker:** Sewer Working Plain Seams (as opposed to Embroidery Work)

- **Plowright:** A Maker of Plows and Other Farm Implements

- **Plumber:** Originally, One Who Installed Lead Roofing or Set Lead Frames for Windows

- **Porter:** Door Keeper

- **Puddler:** Wrought Iron Worker

- **Pumbum Worker:** Plumber

- **Quarrel Picker:** Glass Installer

- **Quarrier:** Quarry Worker

- **Quarryman:** A Stonecutter

- **Quillwright:** Wheelwright

- **Quister:** Worker Who Bleaches Fabric

- **Raker:** A Street Cleaner

- **Rattlewatch:** Town Watchman

- **Resurrectionist:** Someone Who Digs Up Recently Buried Corpses for Use as Cadavers

- **Rigger:** Hoist Tackle Worker

- **Ripper:** Seller of Fish

- **Roper:** Maker of Rope or Nets

- **Saddler:** One Who Makes, Repairs or Sells Saddles or Other Furnishings for Horses

- **Salter:** Roofer

- **Sawbones:** Physician

- **Sawyer:** Lumber Worker or Saw Operator

- **Scavelman:** Cleaner of Ditches

- **Schumacker:** Shoemaker

- **Scriber:** Marker of Measured Bails of Cotton at The Docks

- **Scribler:** A Minor or Worthless Author

- **Scrivener:** Professional or Public Copyist or Writer, or Notary Public

- **Scrutineer:** Election Judge

- **Sempster:** Seamstress

- **Ship Chandler:** Made and Sold 'Fixings' for Ships (Ropes, Shackles, Sailcloth)

- **Shookmaker:** Maker of Shipping Crates and Fruit Boxes

- **Shrieve:** Sheriff

- **Skutcher:** Worker Who Beat Flax to Obtain The Tow Inside for Making Linen

- **Slater:** Roofer

- **Slopseller:** Seller of Ready-Made Clothes in A Slop Shop

- **Snobscat:** Repaired Shoes

- **Solicitor:** City or County Attorney

- **Sorter:** Tailor

- **Spinster:** A Woman Who Spins or An Unmarried Woman

- **Spurrer:** Maker of Spurs

- **Squire:** Country Gentleman, Farm Owner, or Justice of The Peace

- **Stavemaker:** One Who Cut and Bent The "Staves," Narrow, Shaped Strips of Wood That Made A Barrel

- **Stevedore:** A Dockworker

- **Stuffgrownsman (Stuff Gowsman):** Junior Barrister

- **Tanner:** One Who Tans (Cures) Animal Hides Into Leather

- **Tapley:** One Who Puts The Tap in An Ale Cask

- **Tasker:** Reaper

- **Teamster:** One Who Drives A Team for Hauling

- **Tenterer:** Worker Who Would Hang Finished Cloth on Hooks to Dry Before Sale

- **Thatcher:** Roofer

- **Tickneyman:** Traveling Salesman Specializing in Pottery

- **Tide Waiter:** Custom Inspector

- **Tiller:** Farmer

- **Tinker:** Repairer of Pots and Pans

- **Tinsmith:** One Who Makes or Repairs Things Made of Light Metal, Like Tin.

- **Tipper:** Maker of Arrow Tips

- **Tipstaff:** Policeman

- **Topper:** Spinning Mill Worker

- **Tracer:** Drafter Who Traces Designs Using Wax or Trace Paper

- **Travers:** Toll Bridge Collection

- **Treenmaker:** Artisan of Wooden Housewares

- **Tucker:** Cleaner of Cloth Goods

- **Turner:** A Person Who Turns Wood on A Lathe Into Spindles

- **Ulnager:** Woolens Inspector

- **Underviewer or Underlooker:** Mine Supervisor

- **Upright Worker:** Chimney Sweep

- **Vabster:** Weaver

- **Valet:** Personal Assistant to A Wealthy Man

- **Verderer:** Game Warden

- **Victualer:** A Tavern Keeper or One Who Provides An Army, Navy, or Ship with Food

- **Vulcan:** Blacksmith

- **Wagoner:** Teamster Not for Hire

- **Wainwright:** Wagon Maker

- **Waiter:** Customs Officer or Tide Waiter

- **Wakeman:** Night Watchman

- **Warrener:** Gamekeeper and Butcher for The Rabbit Warrens on A Large Estate

- **Waterman:** Boatman Who Plies for Hire

- **Way Maker:** Road Builder

- **Webster:** Operator of Looms

- **Weirkeeper:** A Fish Trapper

- **Wellwright:** Maker of The Gears for Well Mechanisms

- **Wharfinger:** Owner of A Wharf

- **Wheelwright:** One Who Made or Repaired Wheels, Wheeled Carriages

- **Wherryman:** Sailor of A Flat-Bottomed

- **Whitesmith:** Worker of Cool Metals, as Opposed to A Blacksmith.

- **Whitewing:** Street Sweeper

- **Whitster:** Bleacher of Cloth

- **Wright:** Workman, Especially A Construction Worker

- **Wyrth:** Laborer

- **Yagger:** Fish Peddler

- **Yatman:** Gatekeeper

- **Yeoman:** Farmer Who Owns His Own Land

10. Photographs and Physical Description

An old proverb states that
"the eyes are the windows into the soul."
A genealogy corollary is that
"a photo is a window into the lives of your ancestors."

11 Ways That Historical Photos Provide Clues

Historical Photos provide wonderful clues about our ancestors' lives.

- **Clothing:** The clothing that was worn can give us great clues as to the date of the photograph and therefore clues for our research.

- **Furniture and Props:** In a professional photograph – more timing clues.

- **Gravestone Photo:** Terrific birth and death date information (although not always accurate) and whom the person is buried next to or near can provide additional clues.

- **Hair Style:** Clues about the timing of the photo.

- **House Architecture:** Many photos were taken on the outside of a home. I even have many photos where the house number is included. The architecture of the home can provide some clues as to its location.

- **Photo Frame:** Was it in a cardboard frame that often had the photographer's name and city or address?

- **Postcards:** In the first few decades of the 20th century, special postcards with a photo on the back were mailed. Obviously, the writing in the corresponding part of the card can provide great clues.

- **Professional Photographer:** If a professional photographer took the photos, does his name and location or the name of the studio give us a clue as to the ancestor's residence?

- **Surrounding Information:** Such as landscape, signs, furniture, machinery, automobiles, and even technology such as radios and televisions. This can give you dating clues or the location of the photo; in some cases, their residence location or where they went on vacation.

- **Type of Photo:** Daguerreotype? Tintype? Cabinet card? These elements can provide you with timing information.

- **Writing on the back:** Many times, the names of the folks in the photo were written on the back. But since you don't know who wrote the names or when they were written, use caution as to their accuracy.

For the best information regarding dating an old photograph, visit Maureen Taylor's Photo Detective website (MaureenTaylor.com). And in the U.K., Jayne Shrimpton's website (JayneShrimpton.co.uk). Both have numerous articles and books pertinent to photo analysis.

13 Ways to Find Physical Characteristics without Photos

As we all know, there are no photos available for all our ancestors, especially many of those who lived primarily in the 1800s or earlier. On the other hand, we may have photos in our collection in what I call my "Unknowns," where they have not been identified, and may never be identified.

So how do we know what our ancestors looked like if there are no identified photos? Well, there are several artifacts that are available to family historians and genealogists that at least describe their physical characteristics.

Below are 13 examples. I am sure that there are more.

- **Chinese Exclusion Act Case Files:** Physical appearance information was included in the records.

- **Drivers and Other Licenses:** Licenses didn't always have photos but often include height, weight, hair color and eye color.

- **Hospital and Other Medical Records:** Include height, weight, and race.

- **Immigration Records:** In immigration records for specific years, some physical description info was required. In this example, health condition, deformities, height, complexion, eye, and hair color, and identifying marks were required.

- **Military Discharge Records:** There are an abundance of forms in the military, and many of them record physical characteristics. My father's discharge from the Marine Corps included height, eye color, hair color, and complexion were noted.

- **Military Enlistment Records:** Include height, hair and eye color, and complexion

- **Naturalization Records:** There have been a few variations of naturalization forms, but several of them asked for skin color, height, weight, eye, and hair color, as well as distinctive marks.

- **Passport Applications:** Although some applications indeed have photos (although less than high quality), several physical characteristics were requested of the applicant, such as stature, forehead, eye color, nose, mouth, chin, hair color, complexion, face characteristics, and distinguishing marks.

- **Pension Applications:** In pension applications, there often is a place to enter physical characteristics. Examples for a Civil War pension, include a place to enter age, height, weight, complexion, and eye and hair color. In Surgeons Certificates, there is an abundance of health information as well.

- **Prison Records:** The usual age, hair color, height, eye color, physical deformities, and I have seen one that includes temperament!

- **U.S. Customs Service Records:** For seamen, their physical description was included in the records.

- **Voter Registration:** In some voter registration logs, physical characteristic information was requested. In some records, applicants included their age, height, complexion, eye color, hair color as well as marks or scars.

- **World War I or II Draft Cards:** On the second page of the card, questions were asked about the applicant's physical characteristics: height, build, eye color, hair color, physical markings, physical deformities, and in one version whether he was bald.

Notes

11. Residences and Other Locations

"How they lived" is the essence
of the family historian's challenge;
where they lived is the first step to discovery.

32 Ways to Find Ancestor Locations and Addresses

- **Alumni Records and Student Directories:** Generally, include the college student or alumnus' current address in them.

- **Birth Certificates:** The parents address is included, and one is not making a rush to judgment that this same address may be the baby's first residence as well, at least in most cases.

- **Business Correspondence:** Letters, receipts, contracts, and even old business cards include addresses.

- **Cemetery Records:** If the ancestor purchased a cemetery plot, it is likely that the cemetery has a record of the person's address at the time of the purchase.

- **Census Records:** Includes addresses; often written vertically on the left side of the page.

- **City Directories:** Includes telephone directories; Include people's residential and often business addresses Don't forget that they are very useful for business, lodge, associations, and church addresses as well.

- **Court Records:** Most kinds of court records would include the address of your ancestor. Likely candidates are divorces and civil judgments.

- **Death Certificates:** The decedent's address as well as that of the informants are generally included.

- **Draft Cards:** The draftee's address is included and often when asked for a contact person, that person's address is included.

- **Family and Personal Correspondence:** Letters and postcards to and from family members typically included their residence addresses.

- **Immigration and Travel Records:** Post 1900 the address of the traveler is included in travel records and the address of where the immigrant is "going" is included in immigration records.

- **Land, Deed, and Property Records:** After 1860, it is likely that a physical address may be associated with the deed. Later property records include the address.

- **Maps and Atlases:** Generally, do not have people's name on them, but they might. A location might be identified as the "Smith Farm" or the "Johnson General Store". These might be helpful in narrowing down the location, residence, or business of an ancestor.

- **Marriage Announcements in Newspapers:** Marriage license announcements include the bride and groom's addresses. The society pages include parties, visitors, and addresses of the event as well as some participants.

- **Marriage Licenses:** Include the address of the bride and groom. May be on the marriage certificate as well, but more likely in the ledger or register of marriages or other pertinent logbook of the local jurisdiction.

- **Military Records:** If the person was drafted or enlisted, it is likely that their permanent address and that of the next of kin were recorded in their enlistment papers.

- **Miscellaneous Newspaper Articles:** Many list the address of the subject(s) of the article. Don't forget classified ads.

- **Mortuary Records:** The decedent's address is included in the document.

- **Naturalization Records:** The potential citizen's address is specified.

- **Newspaper Legal Notices and Real Estate Transactions:** Likely would include the address of your ancestor.

- **Obituaries:** Some obituaries contain the residence of the deceased.

- **Patents and Patent Applications:** Contain the address of the applicant.

- **Photographs:** Most photographs don't have addresses affixed or handwritten on them, but I have several photos of my ancestors and relatives taken in front of their house, with the house number prominently displayed. Snapshots were often taken at places that they visited, which were generally handwritten on the back of the photo.

Also, sittings for a professional photographer might include the photographer's name and city, providing more clues.

- **Probate Records and Wills:** Generally, contain the address of the people involved.

- **School Records:** Enrollment lists might have the student's address.

- **Social Security Application:** Contains the address of the applicant.

- **Special Marriage Documents:** Such as marriage banns, bonds, contracts, consent papers, dowries, etc. are likely to have address information.

- **SSDI:** The Social Security Death Index contains the county and state where the last benefits were distributed.

- **Tax Records:** Generally, don't have the person's address, but they might, especially if the taxation pertains to property holdings of your ancestor.

- **The U.S. Public Records Index** is an online compilation that includes addresses from Public Records from as early as 1950. Although these provide clues, their accuracy is often questionable, but worth the effort if you have little success elsewhere.

- **Veteran's Benefit or Pension Record:** Would include the address at time of enlistment, and possibly their current address where they are receiving benefits. If they were deceased, their beneficiaries address would be available.

- **Voting Registration and Great Registers:** The address of the registered voter is included.

Find State of Residence from Social Security Number

You can quickly determine the state of residence by looking up the first three digits of Social Security Number in the data list below. This was very accurate years ago, but there are many cases when the location determined from the first three numbers is not equivalent to the person's residential location. First, here's some information about Social Security.

Generally, if you wish to find out information about an individual's Social Security application, you will need to acquire that person's SS-5 form (ssa.gov/forms/ssa-711.pdf), a photocopy of which can be obtained from the Social Security Administration for a fee of $21.00. See SS-5 Form for the form itself and mailing instructions. The information included on the application is:

- **Full name**
- **Full name at birth** (including maiden name)
- **Present mailing address**
- **Age at last birthday**
- **Date of birth**
- **Place of birth** (city, county, state)
- **Father's full name** "regardless of whether living or dead"
- **Mother's full name**, including maiden name, "regardless of whether living or dead"
- **Sex and race**
- **Ever applied for SS number/Railroad Retirement before?** Yes/No
- **Current employer's name and address**
- **Date signed**
- **Applicant's signature**

But what if you just wish to determine by the actual Social Security Number where the card was issued? In other words, where the applicant was living when they applied? The first 3 digits are called the Area Number, and it provides a clue. From the SSA (ssa.gov) in their description of the Area Number:

"The Area Number is assigned by the geographical region. Prior to 1972, cards were issued in local Social Security offices around the country and the Area Number represented the State in which the card was issued. **This did not necessarily have to be the State where the applicant lived**, since a person could apply for their card in any Social Security office. Since 1972, when SSA began assigning SSNs and issuing cards centrally from Baltimore, the **area number assigned has been based on the ZIP code in the mailing address provided on the application** for the original Social Security card. The applicant's mailing address does not have to be the same as their place of residence. Thus, the Area Number does not necessarily represent the state of residence of the applicant, either prior to 1972 or since."

Also, randomization of numbers started in 2011, so for applications after that date the Area Number has no meaning.

For the great majority of applicants, however, the first 3 digits (Area Number) do represent the state of residence at the time that the application was submitted

On the next page is a list of states and territories and the numbers that represent that location when assigning the SSN, the first 3 digits representing the Area Number, the magical first 3 digits of the SSN. When there is a blank State Name, it means that the state above has received additional numbers.

Please remember that this information only provides clues for your research. Of course, there can be mistakes in the SSA's records. But remember this also, the Area Number has nothing to do with where the applicant was born.

- When the Area Number does have meaning, it refers to where the applicant went to a local office prior to 1972 and the location of that office.

- After 1972, there were additional numbers assigned for each state

- After 2011, the Area Number was randomized, so it ceased to have any meaning.

Furthermore, in current times, Social Security Numbers are often assigned in the hospital of birth.

The following data is current as of 2003.

- **001-003:** New Hampshire

- **004-007:** Maine

- **008-009:** Vermont

- **010-034:** Massachusetts

- **035-039:** Rhode Island

- **040-049:** Connecticut

- **050-134:** New York

- **135-158:** New Jersey

- **159-211:** Pennsylvania

- **212-220:** Maryland

- **221-222:** Delaware

- **223-231:** Virginia

- **691-699:** _____

- **232-236:** West Virginia

- **232:** North Carolina

- **237-246:** _____

- **681-690:** _____

- **247-251:** South Carolina

- **654-658:** _____
- **252-260:** Georgia
- **667-675:** _____
- **261-267:** Florida
- **589-595:** _____
- **766-772:** _____
- **268-302:** Ohio
- **303-317:** Indiana
- **318-361:** Illinois
- **362-386:** Michigan
- **387-399:** Wisconsin
- **400-407:** Kentucky
- **408-415:** Tennessee
- **756-763:** _____
- **416-424:** Alabama
- **425-428:** Mississippi
- **587-588:** _____
- **752-755:** _____
- **429-432:** Arkansas
- **676-679:** _____
- **433-439:** Louisiana
- **659-665:** _____
- **440-448:** Oklahoma
- **449-467:** Texas
- **627-645:** _____
- **468-477:** Minnesota

- **478-485:** Iowa

- **486-500:** Missouri

- **501-502:** North Dakota

- **503-504:** South Dakota

- **505-508:** Nebraska

- **509-515:** Kansas

- **516-517:** Montana

- **518-519:** Idaho

- **520:** Wyoming

- **521-524:** Colorado

- **650-653:** _____

- **525,585:** New Mexico

- **648-649:** _____

- **526-527:** Arizona

- **600-601:** _____

- **764-765:** _____

- **528-529:** Utah

- **646-647:** _____

- **530:** Nevada

- **680:** _____

- **531-539:** Washington

- **540-544:** Oregon

- **545-573:** California

- **602-626:** _____

- **574:** Alaska

- **575-576:** Hawaii

- **750-751:** _____

- **577-579:** District of Columbia

- **580:** Virgin Islands

- **580-584:** Puerto Rico

- **596-599:** _____

- **586:** Guam

- **586:** American Samoa

- **586:** Philippine Islands

- **700-728:** Railroad Board

- **729-733:** Enumeration at Entry

12. Schools and Yearbooks

Discovering your ancestor's first life interests
can often be found in Yearbooks.

11 Things You Can Find by Researching Alumni Records

Maybe it's just me, but I have never heard anyone write or talk about using Alumni Records in their genealogy research. I use them personally and have discovered mountains of information in these gems.

I contend that alumni records are part directories, part newspapers and magazines, part biographies, part obituaries, part yearbooks, part vital records, etc. You get the idea. If you are seeking genealogy clues, these "records' are full of them. All the information is derivative, but it can provide leads for you to search for original documents. And if you are documenting a person's family story, well, there's a ton of that kind of information too.

So, what am I including in Alumni Records?

- Alumni directories

- Alumni registers

- Alumni newsletters, bulletins, newspapers, and magazines

- Commencement programs

- Alumni Association records

And what information is available in them?

- Graduation dates and degree(s) received

- Current photos and/or those of their family

- Current address lists

- Where are they now and what are they doing?

- Obituaries and "In Memoriam"

- Marriages

- Children born to the alumnus

- Deaths in their family

- Life achievements and awards

- Interesting stories about the alumnus and their family

- Class reunion memorabilia

19 Places Where You Can Access Old Yearbooks Online

School yearbooks, which immortalize how we looked and what we did in high school or college. Whether we looked goofy or cool, that photo is there forever. And they document what clubs, sports, or other activities we were involved in. And for our ancestors, too!

- **Ancestry.com** has a nice school yearbook collection to search. I would encourage you to check out the schools and years available in the "Browse This Collection" section on the right side of the page to look for a specific yearbook. Ancestry requires a subscription. They have over 450,000 yearbooks – that's yearbooks, not schools.

- **MyHeritage.com** has a huge collection of yearbooks that can be searched. Thy have over 250,000 yearbooks, again yearbooks, not schools. They also have the Alumni Lists originally provided by Distant Cousin. Some are transcribed and some are scanned page images. My Heritage requires a subscription. **WorldVitalRecords.com**, (owned by My Heritage), has 115 schools.

- The last "big player" is **Classmates.com**, which has a collection of over 350,000 yearbooks where a reprint can be purchased. I will leave it up to you to figure out how to save an image or two. It can be accomplished. You can view the yearbooks by browsing. You do not need to have a subscription, but you are limited as to how many pages that you can view.

- **TheAncestorHunt.com** has yearbook links from 12,700 schools in the U.S. and Canada. This information is free.

- The Internet Archive at **Archive.org** has over 66,000 results if you search for the keyword "yearbooks". Worth searching if you know the school or association. By and large, the Internet Archive yearbooks are included in The Ancestor Hunt's list of links.

- **E-Yearbook.com** has a sizable collection available by subscription. You can view by registering. They don't advertise the number of yearbooks, but it is sizable. They also have a nice collection of Military Yearbooks, and Navy Cruise books.

- **Skalooza.com** is interesting. It has a good number of yearbooks available; it is easy to register, and the interface is easy to use. Quite honestly, I have had difficulty finding things on this site.

- The **Old-Yearbooks.com** collection is a combination of scanned and transcribed. It is a combination of class lists, random class pictures, and a list of links, many that are to Classmates.

- **DeadFred.com** has a collection of photos from old yearbooks that you might want to browse.

- **DonsList.net** has a nice collection of old yearbooks and alumni association directories, many from Pittsburgh and Pennsylvania. There are over 100 schools.

- **Ebay.com** and **Amazon.com** have a lot of old yearbooks for sale.

- **GenealogyToday.com** has over 1,700 yearbooks and is a subscription only service.

- There are a few link only sites, such as **CyndisList.com**, **Linkpendium.com**, and **Access Genealogy.com**. The number of links are in the low hundreds, although it is difficult to know Linkpendium's.

- Google Books at **Books.Google.com** has a wide variety of yearbooks available. Many are from an association and are not related to schools. Worth a search. Unfortunately. Most are not viewable.

- **Hathitrust.org** has a couple hundred full view school yearbooks. Usually there are only a couple of years available, and many are in the early 1900s.

26 Things That You Can Find in School Records

Do you research school records? I'm not talking about yearbooks. I'm talking about actual school records, such as enrollment, attendance, and grade reports for example. These are interesting source documents because they might record the students age, birth date and location, and possibly their parents' names. All great ways to find this information if you haven't found them in other documents about your target ancestor. Besides, finding out your grandmother's grades would be interesting!

So, what types of records related to schools are maintained and often available?

- **Academic Team and Class Photos**

- **Alumni Directories and Publications**

- **Attendance Records**

- **Class Logs**

- **Local Newspaper Articles:**

- **Report Cards**

- **School Board Meetings/Reports**

- **School Catalogs**

- **School Census**

- **Student Newspapers**

- **Teacher Rosters**

- **Teacher's Registers**

  - Graduation Lists

  - School Activities

  - School Sports

- **Yearbooks** and **Yearbook Indexes**

And, what type of information can you derive from these school records?

- **Activities** (from Photos)

- **Age**

- **Birth Date**

- **Classes Taken**

- **Current Residence Address**

- **Date Left School** (can help with family residence relocation)

- **Grades**

- **Name of Father**

- **Name of Mother**

- **Name** (often includes middle name which is useful)

- **Occupations of Parents**

- **Physical Characteristics**, such as color/race, disability

Notes

13. Resources

Helpful tips from other websites

Top Websites

The resources that are listed in this section are separated by the type(s) of genealogy records that they correspond to. I have selected three prominent and very useful websites to serve as the primary resources that the reader should visit for any category of interest. For specific resource categories, there may be additional resources listed. Here is an overview of each.

The FamilySearch Wiki

The FamilySearch Research Wiki (www.FamilySearch.org/en/about) is a free, online genealogical guide created and maintained by FamilySearch, a non-profit organization. It contains links to genealogy databases, websites, other resources, research strategies, and genealogical guidance to assist in the search for your ancestors. Articles included are locality pages for countries around the world and topic pages that include pertinent genealogy record types explaining how to use the record, what it contains, and how to find it. It currently has about 100,000 articles.

By and large, the Wiki is organized by location first. Although there are references to collections around the world, the resources described and referenced below will be for the United States. However, much of the descriptive material about certain record types transcends location.

Cyndi's List

- A categorized & cross-referenced index to genealogical resources on the Internet.

- A list of links that point you to genealogical research sites online.

- A free jumping-off point for you to use in your online research.

- A "card catalog" to the genealogical collection in the immense library that is the Internet.

- Your genealogical research portal onto the Internet.

- Cyndi's List currently has over 315,000 links in about 230 categories and sub-categories

The Ancestor Hunt

The Ancestor Hunt provides a list of links to free online record collections in 20 different major genealogy categories. Unlike the FamilySearch Wiki, and Cyndi's List, The Ancestor Hunt does not have subcategories. The Ancestor Hunt also has articles about genealogy research and tools and techniques to enhance one's ability to be successful in their research.

Currently it has over 160,000 links to Free Online Record Collections in the U.S. and Canada.

Starting Your Genealogy Research Journey

- Start Your Genealogy Research
  www.Archives.gov/research/genealogy/start-research

- New to Genealogy - Beginners First Step
  www.FamilySearch.org/wiki/en/New_to_Genealogy_-_Beginners_First_Step

- 10 Steps to Start Building Your Family Tree
  www.FamilyTreeMagazine.com/general-genealogy/10-steps-to-start

- How to Begin Tracing Your Family Tree
  www.thoughtco.com/how-to-trace-your-family-tree-1420458

Alumni Records

- Cyndi's List – Schools > Alumni Organizations & Resources
  CyndisList.com/schools/alumni

- The Ancestor Hunt – Alumni Records
  TheAncestorHunt.com/alumni-records.html

Birth Records

- FamilySearch Wiki – Wiki – Vital Records > Birth Records
  www.FamilySearch.org/wiki/en/United_States_Birth_Records

- Cyndi's List – Births & Baptisms
  CyndisList.com/births

- The Ancestor Hunt – Births
  TheAncestorHunt.com/births.html

Cemetery Records

- FamilySearch Wiki – United States > Cemeteries
  www.FamilySearch.org/wiki/en/United_States_Cemeteries

- Cyndi's List – Cemeteries & Funeral Homes
  CyndisList.com/cemeteries

- The Ancestor Hunt – Cemetery Records
  TheAncestorHunt.com/cemetery-records.html

- A Gravesite Can Reveal Remarkable Details About Your Ancestor, IF You
  Can Find It: Here's How
  FamilyHistoryDaily.com/genealogy-help-and-how-to/find-a-gravesite

- Rootsweb – Cemetery Records
  wiki.RootsWeb.com/wiki/index.php/Cemetery_Records

Church Records

- FamilySearch Wiki – United States > Church Records
  www.FamilySearch.org/wiki/en/United_States_Church_Records

- Cyndi's List – Religion & Churches
  CyndisList.com/religion

- The Ancestor Hunt - Church Records
  TheAncestorHunt.com/church-records.html

- Random Acts of Genealogical Kindness (RAOGK) > U.S. Church Records Research Guide
  raogk.org/church-records

- A Genealogist's Guide to Using Catholic Records in Genealogy Research
  www.LegacyTree.com/blog/catholic-records-genealogy-research

City Directories

- FamilySearch Wiki – United States > Directories
  www.FamilySearch.org/wiki/en/United_States_Directories

- FamilySearch Wiki – Canada > Directories
  www.FamilySearch.org/wiki/en/Canada_Directories

- Cyndi's List – Directories: City, County, Address, etc.
  CyndisList.com/directories

- The Ancestor Hunt – Directories
  TheAncestorHunt.com/directories.html

- How to Use City Directories In Your Genealogy Research
  LisaLisson.com/how-to-use-city-directories-in-your-genealogy-research

- What's In a City Directory? (A 10-article series about City Directories)
  CreativeGene.blogspot.com/2007/05/whats-in-city-directory.html

- Where to Find City Directories Online
  www.TheAncestorHunt.com/blog/where-to-find-city-directories-online

Coroner Records

- Cyndi's List – Coroners & Medical Examiners
  CyndisList.com/coroners

- The Ancestor Hunt – Coroner Records
  TheAncestorHunt.com/coroner-records.html

Death Records

- FamilySearch Wiki – United States > Vital Records > Death Records
  www.FamilySearch.org/wiki/en/United_States_Death_Records

- Cyndi's List – Death Records
  CyndisList.com/death

- The Ancestor Hunt – Deaths
  TheAncestorHunt.com/deaths.html

Divorce Records

- FamilySearch Wiki – United States > Vital Records > Divorce Records
  www.FamilySearch.org/wiki/en/United_States_Divorce_Records

- Cyndi's List – Marriages and Divorce
  CyndisList.com/marriages

- The Ancestor Hunt – Divorce Records
  TheAncestorHunt.com/divorce-records.html

Immigration Records

- FamilySearch Wiki – United States > Emigration and Immigration
  www.FamilySearch.org/wiki/en/United_States_Emigration_and_Immigration

- Cyndi's List - Immigration, Emigration & Migration
  CyndisList.com/immigration

- The Ancestor Hunt - Immigration and Travel Records
  TheAncestorHunt.com/immigration.html

- National Archives Immigration Records
  www.Archives.gov/research/immigration/overview

- U.S. Immigration Records Research Guide: Passenger Lists, Naturalization, and More
  www.FamilySearch.org/blog/en/immigration-records-research-guide

- American Family Immigration History Center and Research Ellis Island
  www.StatueOfLiberty.org/ellis-island/family-history-center

Marriage Records

- FamilySearch Wiki – United States > Vital Records > Marriage Records
  www.FamilySearch.org/wiki/en/United_States_Marriage_Records

- Cyndi's List – Marriages and Divorce
  CyndisList.com/marriages

- The Ancestor Hunt – Marriages
  TheAncestorHunt.com/marriages.html

Military Records

- FamilySearch Wiki – United States > Military Records
  www.FamilySearch.org/wiki/en/United_States_Military_Records

- Cyndi's List – Military Worldwide
  CyndisList.com/military-worldwide

- The Ancestor Hunt
  TheAncestorHunt.com/military-records.html

Mortuary Records

- FamilySearch Wiki – United States > Funeral Home Records
  www.FamilySearch.org/wiki/en/United_States_Funeral_Home_Records

- Cyndi's List – Cemeteries & Funeral Homes > Funeral Home & Mortuary Records
  CyndisList.com/cemeteries/funeral-home-records

- The Ancestor Hunt – Mortuary Records
  TheAncestorHunt.com/mortuary-records.html

- Finding Funeral Home Records for Your Ancestors
  www.LegacyTree.com/blog/finding-ancestor-funeral-home-records

- Funeral Home Records: Telling Stories of the Dearly Departed
  www.Trace.com/genealogists/2018/01/funeral-home-records-telling-stories-dearly-departed

Naturalization Records

- FamilySearch Wiki – United States > Naturalization and Citizenship
  www.FamilySearch.org/wiki/en/United_States_Naturalization_and_Citizenship

- Cyndi's List – Naturalization & Citizenship
  CyndisList.com/naturalization

- The Ancestor Hunt – Naturalization Records
  TheAncestorHunt.com/naturalization-records.html

- The U.S. Archives Naturalization Records
  www.Archives.gov/research/naturalization/naturalization.html

- Women and Naturalization
  www.Archives.gov/publications/prologue/1998/summer/women-and-naturalization-1.html

Newspapers

- FamilySearch Wiki – United States > Newspapers
  www.FamilySearch.org/wiki/en/United_States_Newspapers

- Cyndi's List – Newspapers
  CyndisList.com/newspapers

- The Ancestor Hunt – Newspapers - Articles About Newspaper Research
  TheAncestorHunt.com/newspapers.html

- The Ancestor Hunt – Newspaper Links – Free Online Historical Newspapers
  TheAncestorHunt.com/newspaper-research-links.html

Obituaries

- FamilySearch Wiki – United States – Obituaries
  www.FamilySearch.org/wiki/en/United_States_Obituaries

- Cyndi's List – Obituaries
  CyndisList.com/obituaries

- The Ancestor Hunt – Obituaries
  TheAncestorHunt.com/obituaries.html

- How to Find Historical Obituaries
  www.TheAncestorHunt.com/blog/how-to-find-historical-obituaries

- What is the Future of Obituaries?
  www.TheAncestorHunt.com/blog/what-is-the-future-of-obituaries

- What is the Difference between an Obituary, a Death Notice, an
  Obituary Index, and a Death Index?
  www.TheAncestorHunt.com/blog/what-is-the-difference-between-an-
  obituary-a-death-notice-an-obituary-index-and-a-death-index

Photos

- Cyndi's List – Photographs & Memories
  CyndisList.com/photos

- The Ancestor Hunt – Photos
  TheAncestorHunt.com/photos.html

- Maureen Taylor – The Photo Detective
  MaureenTaylor.com

- Jayne Shrimpton - UK-based professional dress historian, portrait
  specialist and 'photo detective' since the 1980s.
  www.JayneShrimpton.co.uk

- Dead Fred Genealogy Photo Archive
  www.DeadFred.com

- Ancient Faces
  www.AncientFaces.com

Probate Records and Wills

- FamilySearch Wiki – United States > Probate Records
  www.FamilySearch.org/wiki/en/United_States_Probate_Records

- Cyndi's List – Wills & Probate
  CyndisList.com/wills

- The Ancestor Hunt – Probate and Wills
  TheAncestorHunt.com/probate-and-wills.html

- Wills and Probate Records are Genealogy Riches
  LisaLouiseCooke.com/2018/01/31/wills-probate-records-genealogy

- How to Use Wills and Estate Records to Learn About Your Ancestors
  www.ThoughtCo.com/probing-into-probate-records-1420839

- Probate Records Could Be the Key to Unlocking Your Family's Hidden Past
  FamilyHistoryDaily.com/genealogy-help-and-how-to/probate-records-genealogy

School Records

- FamilySearch Wiki – United States > School Records
  www.FamilySearch.org/wiki/en/United_States_School_Records

- Cyndi's List – Schools
  CyndisList.com/schools

- The Ancestor Hunt – School Records
  TheAncestorHunt.com/school-records.html

- 5 Quick Tips to Get the Most Out of Education Records
  www.FindMyPast.com/blog/family-records/5-quick-tips-to-get-the-most-out-of-education-records

- Top 10 Strategies for Finding School Records for Genealogy
  LisaLouiseCooke.com/2019/10/29/school-records-for-genealogy

- Getting Started With School Records for Genealogy Research
  LisaLisson.com/getting-started-with-school-records-for-genealogy-research

Voter Records

- FamilySearch Wiki – United States > Voting Records
  www.FamilySearch.org/wiki/en/United_States_Voting_Records

- Cyndi's List – Voters, Poll Books, Electoral Records
  CyndisList.com/voters

- The Ancestor Hunt – Voter Records
  TheAncestorHunt.com/voter-lists.html

- How to Trace Your Ancestors in Voter Records
  www.FamilyTreeMagazine.com/us/tracing-ancestors-in-voter-records

- Digging Deeper: Voter Registrations
  DevilsLakendLibrary.com/wp-content/uploads/2019/03/Digging-Deeper-Voter-Registrations.pdf

Yearbooks

- FamilySearch Wiki – Unite States > School Records > Yearbooks
  www.FamilySearch.org/wiki/en/United_States_School_Records

- Cyndi's List – Schools > Yearbooks and Annuals
  CyndisList.com/schools/yearbooks

- The Ancestor Hunt – Yearbooks
  TheAncestorHunt.com/yearbooks.html

- Using Yearbooks For Genealogical Research
  news.LegacyFamilyTree.com/legacy_news/2016/10/using-yearbooks-for-genealogical-research-.html

- A Genealogy Education is in School Yearbooks
  www.RecordClick.com/a-genealogy-education-school-yearbook-memories

- Genealogy 101: School Yearbooks
  blog.GenealogyBank.com/genealogy-101-school-yearbooks.html

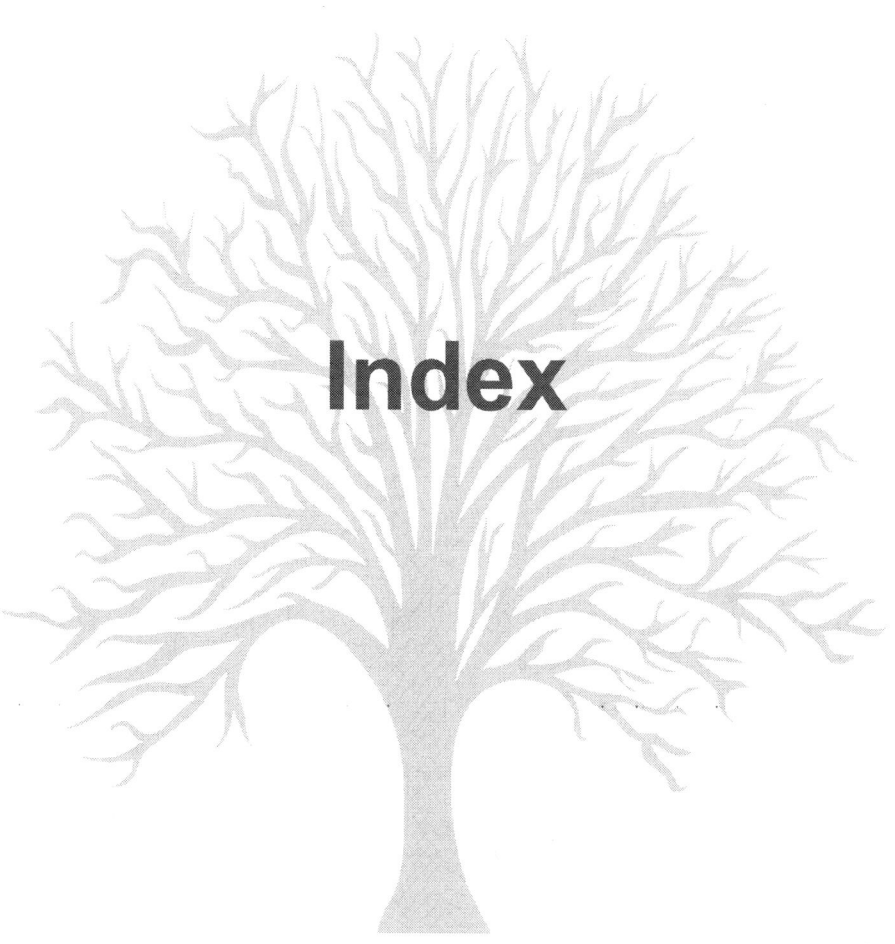

Index

A Quick Reference for Common Search Terms

V

W

Y

Notes